# LAUDONNIERE
# & FORT CAROLINE

# LAUDONNIERE
# & FORT CAROLINE

*History and Documents*

## CHARLES E. BENNETT

## THE UNIVERSITY OF ALABAMA PRESS
*Tuscaloosa*

Copyright © 2001
The University of Alabama Press
Tuscaloosa, Alabama 35487-0380
All rights reserved
Manufactured in the United States of America

Originally published by The University of
Florida Press in 1964.

9 8 7 6 5 4 3 2 1
10 09 08 07 06 05 04 03 02 01

∞

The paper on which this book is printed meets
the minimum requirements of American
National Standard for Information Science-
Permanence of Paper for Printed Library
Materials, ANSI Z39.48-1984.

CIP information is available from
the Library of Congress.

ISBN   978-0-8173-1122-3  (pbk. : alk.  paper)
       978-0-8173-8338-1  (electronic)

DEDICATED TO
THE MOST PERFECT WOMEN I HAVE EVER KNOWN
*MY MOTHER & MY WIFE*

# FOREWORD TO PAPERBACK EDITION
Jerald T. Milanich

America's history was shaped in part by the clash of cultures that took place in the southeastern United States in the 1560s. Indians, French, and Spaniards vied to profit from European attempts to colonize the land Juan Ponce de Leon had named *La Florida*. It was a decade of decisive actions, which, though played out largely along the coast of South Carolina, Georgia, and Florida, were closely tied to geopolitics on the opposite side of the Atlantic Ocean.

Prior to the publication of *Laudonnière & Fort Caroline* little scholarly attention had been focused on the role of the French in those early colonization efforts. The events of four centuries ago were little known by the general public whose knowledge of American history began with the English at Jamestown in 1607. With this book, Charles E. Bennett, would change all that.

Charles E. Bennett is one of the more interesting people one would ever want to meet. A veteran of World War II, he represented northeast Florida in the U. S. House of Representatives for decades. Devoted to his region, Congressman Bennett was highly successful in garnering federal support for his constituency. He also brought them something that was priceless: their history. It was through his efforts that Fort Caroline National Memorial was established. Fort Caroline, of course, is the name the French christened their small settlement founded in 1564 on the south bank of the St. Johns River near Jacksonville.

Bennett next set out to pen the story of that French Huguenot settlement, its colonists' interactions with the Timucua Indians who were native to the region, and the capture of Fort Caroline in 1565 by Spaniards led by Pedro Menéndez de Avilés. That military encounter resulted in the establishment of St. Augustine, assuring La Florida would remain in Spanish hands for many years to come.

Bennett's research is based on documents found in the archives of France and Spain. In the second part of the book he provides translations of many of those accounts. They contain descriptions of Native Americans and the natural wonders of the land in which they lived, information crucial to our present knowledge of the Timucua Indians.

This is a classic book, written by a person who himself is a classic. I am honored to be a part of the University of Alabama Press's initiative to put this important volume back in print.

# PREFACE

HERE are striking similarities between the sixteenth and twentieth centuries. Four hundred years ago the major states of Western Europe vied for headship in exploring and settling the unknown parts of the world. Today the most powerful nations of the earth compete in probing the mysteries of space. In the sixteenth century man was seeking the means to break chains that limited his freedom; in the twentieth century some men still yearn for freedom, while in the free world other men strive to protect their liberties from "isms" which would restrict them. In both centuries the cruelties of mankind dishonored God, but in both centuries new ideas and new ways of doing things gave promise of a brighter tomorrow.

Before 1500, Portuguese and Spanish captains had sailed south around Africa to the Orient and west to the Caribbean Islands. During the first decades of the sixteenth century, Spanish conquistadors explored and established colonies in Central America, Mexico, and South America. They found gold and silver there, and they searched for precious metals in areas which are now parts of the United States. With the sanction of the Pope, Portugal and Spain divided the "unknown world" between themselves and attempted to exclude settlers of other countries from their assigned lands; but England, France, and the Netherlands refused either to admit the right of the Pope to divide the world between Portugal and Spain or to recognize the monopoly claimed by the Iberian countries. Sea captains backed by England and France platted the coasts and harbors of North America. But international war and internal conflicts prevented England and France from attempting settlements in the New World until the second half of the sixteenth century.

*Almost every American student has the opportunity to read of the great explorers—Columbus, Vasco da Gama, Ponce de León, Magellan, Cortez, Pizarro, De Soto, the Cabots, Cartier, and Henry Hudson—but few history textbooks record the activities of Jean Ribault in Florida. Fewer still give Laudonnière credit for leading French colonists to North America and planting a colony in Florida. The principal subject of this book, its text and documents, is René de Goulaine de Laudonnière of France. In 1564 he established a French colony at Fort Caroline on the banks of the St. Johns River and governed his often discontented colonists for more than a year. In his later years he asked: "Shall I, Laudonnière, pass away untouched by glory?"[1] A companion of his at Fort Caroline described the perilous passage from France to Florida as a "road, wonderfully strange."[2] Wonderfully strange too is the life of Laudonnière. In a sense he was untouched by glory. His destiny was not to found the first permanent European colony within the present limits of the United States, but his settlement did activate Spain and did result in the establishment of St. Augustine, the oldest city in the United States. He thus in fact began the permanent settlement of our country. Furthermore, Laudonnière was the first man to lead peculiarly dedicated men and women to North America—colonists searching for a place where they could worship God according to the dictates of their conscience. This French leader deserves a more important place in the annals of the past than that which historians have assigned him.*

*A statue in Washington bears the inscription "What is past is prologue." While this idea is sufficient justification for the study of history, there are other valid reasons for investigating the heritage of mankind. Knowledge and understanding of human experience should prevent modern man from repeating the mistakes of his ancestors, and a study of their civilization should enable him to act with intelligence and plan for the future. For instance, a study of the political intrigues of Queen Mother Catherine de Medici and other politicos of France in the 1560's and of the conflict between Catholics and Protestants in that country should prepare citizens of the United States to understand many current problems and to solve them by considered action. The tyranny of the sixteenth cen-*

tury has been supplanted in the free world by democratic proc-
esses in which the rights of individuals are protected, and concerted
action by the free people of the world can eliminate the islands of
tyranny existing in this modern age.

Four hundred years ago Laudonnière and hundreds of his
French compatriots sought religious freedom on what became the
shores of America. They stepped upward to a new and higher plateau in man's ageless search for freedom. A little more than two
hundred years later, the American Revolution created a country
dedicated to upholding the right of all men to be free and, thereby,
another more lofty plateau of liberty was attained. Today, almost
two hundred years after the writing of the Declaration of Independence and the Constitution of the United States, and four hundred
years after the founding of Fort Caroline, Americans have vowed
not only to preserve their freedom but also to assist mankind all
over the rest of the world in his struggle against those individuals
or nations that would keep him in bondage or re-enslave him. A
high plane of personal liberty and responsibility is within the grasp
of the freedom-loving people of the earth. On the other hand, ignorance of the past and refusal to act with intelligent concern can
turn mankind back to dictatorships over mind and body, thus re-
establishing the restrictive despotism of past centuries. By strange
coincidence, Americans of today are seeking new worlds in space
from the launching pads at the John F. Kennedy Space Center—
at Cape Canaveral near where the French settled in 1564. Too often
historians concentrate on the great men and neglect the people of
little fame. Though he won no more than limited recognition from
his generation, Laudonnière helped turn the tide of history in the
right direction.

This book is the result of thirty years of interest and study. In
the preparation of the manuscript, source materials in Latin, Italian, French, and Spanish were read and translated. Insofar as the
author knows, most of the documents, depositions, and articles in
the second part of this volume appear in English for the first time.
The author is grateful to the excellent staff at the Library of Congress—particularly to Elisabeth Hanunian, Tom V. Wilder, and
William Springer—for checking his translations and for many

*other helpful aids. For the inspiration to begin this study, he is es-
pecially indebted to two citizens of Jacksonville, Florida, and historians of note: the late T. Frederick Davis and the charming,
active Carita Doggett Corse. For encouragement in the effort to produce this book and for careful and constructive suggestions and an
infinite amount of hard work, he is deeply indebted to his friend
Dr. Rembert W. Patrick, a distinguished historian on the faculty of
the University of Florida.*

CHARLES E. BENNETT

# CONTENTS

FOREWORD TO PAPERBACK EDITION—PAGE VI

PREFACE—PAGE VII

ILLUSTRATIONS—PAGE XIV

THE FIRST PART—THE HISTORY

I—PAGE 3
*New Horizons*

II—PAGE 7
*The "Dog" Violates the Law of Kingdoms and Christianity*

III—PAGE 12
*Exploring Florida with Ribault*

IV—PAGE 17
*Threshold of Freedom—America's Beginnings*

V—PAGE 33
*Succor and Massacre*

VI—PAGE 45
*"The Countess" Saves the Captain*

VII—PAGE 53
*Remember Me, Remember David*

NOTES—PAGE 59

THE SECOND PART—THE DOCUMENTS

PAGE 63
*What They Said*

I—PAGE 65
*Maytime*

II—PAGE 71
Concerning Flying Alligators

III—PAGE 76
*The Sea Hath Nothing Greater*

IV—PAGE 79
Stranger Things Are Yet to Come

V—PAGE 87
*Deposition of Robert Meleneche*

VI—PAGE 94
*Deposition of Stefano de Rojomonte*

VII—PAGE 99
*Deposition of Jehan Mamyn, Seaman*

VIII—PAGE 103
*Deposition of Francisco Ruiz Manso*

IX—PAGE 107
*Report of Manrique de Rojas*

X—PAGE 125
*Menéndez and Fort Caroline*

XI—PAGE 141
*Memoire of the Happy Result*

XII—PAGE 164
*Poems of Le Challeux*

XIII—PAGE 166
*The Petition of the Widows and Orphans of Fort Caroline*

XIV—PAGE 171
*Chief Saturiba, Ally*

XV—PAGE 177
*The Signature of Laudonnière*

APPENDIX A—PAGE 179
*The Heavens Direct*

APPENDIX B—PAGE 186
*Sixteenth Century Plant Life in Florida*

Index—PAGE 189

# ILLUSTRATIONS

PAGE VI

Map of Florida in 1565, showing Cape Canaveral


PAGE 2

Laudonnière—apparently a 19th century adaptation of the original
Le Moyne drawing


PAGE 8

A 16th century map of Brittany


PAGE 15

View of Dieppe in 1600


PAGE 18

View of 16th century (1563) Havre-de-Grâce


PAGE 20

A 16th century illustration of bison in Florida


PAGE 24

Placer mining for gold by Indians (La Moyne)

XIV

PAGE 32

Monstrous beast of Florida


PAGE 58

Laudonnière's "French Florida"


PAGE 62

Le Moyne's Map of Florida


PAGE 69

Plan of Fort Caroline (1564)


PAGE 77

Laudonnière portrait, with inscription


PAGE 92

An 18th century Spanish map of Florida


PAGE 140

A 16th century soldier


PAGE 172

Saturiba, Laudonnière's ally


PAGE 177

Laudonnière's only known signature


PAGE 180

A 16th century astrolabe

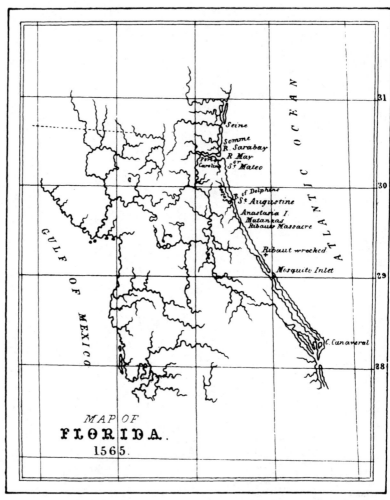

MAP OF
FLORIDA.
1565.

George R. Fairbanks, *The History and Antiquities of the City of St. Augustine*
(New York: C. B. Norton, 1858)

Reproduced from the Collections of the Library of Congress.

THE FIRST PART

# THE HISTORY

Laudonnière.

Léon Guérin, *Les Navigateurs francais* (Paris, Bertrand, 1847)

# I

# *New Horizons*

HE sixteenth century was not a time for trifles. Important people, both good and evil, marched through its decades and left their impress upon its image. History records the achievements and the failures of its famous and infamous men and women, but magnificent accomplishments were made by some individuals whose greatness went unheralded and almost unrecorded. Sixteenth century Frenchmen benefited from the changes which had taken place in Western Europe. Although vestiges remained of old and restrictive economic systems, manorial agriculture with its emphasis on custom and practice was almost supplanted by improved methods of cultivation, and towns and guilds gave men some freedom in the choice of occupation. Merchants and guild masters protected their vested interests by upholding the status quo and decrying change; but the spirit of economic freedom led many Frenchmen into the domestic system of production, free enterprise, and embryonic capitalism.

Trade and the growth of cities doomed feudalism. Traders and burgers demanded uniform laws for large geographic areas, fair-minded judges to interpret the laws, and capable officials to enforce them. The rising middle class supported kings who could control capricious feudal lords. By increasing their power and domain, the kings of Portugal and Spain created states, and those of France and England followed the lead of their Iberian rivals.

A monarch's resources enabled him to seize the opportunity afforded by an adventuresome sea captain. King John I of Portugal subsidized the work of Prince Henry the Navigator, and Ferdinand and Isabella of Spain sent Columbus on his historic voyage. England's Henry VII supported John and Sebastian Cabot in their explorations of North America. Not wanting to be outdone by his

3

neighbors, Francis I of France financed Giovanni da Verrazano and Jacques Cartier in their explorations of the coast of North America from Cape Fear to the St. Lawrence River. Spain, however, first colonized the New World, and by 1550 her colonists lived in the Caribbean Islands, Mexico, Central and South America.

Perhaps the Age of Discovery was one offshoot of the Renaissance, an intellectual rebirth which had liberated the minds of many Europeans. Freed from numerous superstitions, the educated European probed the mysteries of mind and matter. He discovered the vastness of the universe and turned his thoughts to man's relationship with man and with his Creator. In various localities authors wrote in the vernacular, or language of the people, rather than in Latin which relatively few people could read or understand. Scholars translated the Bible into these common languages, and the invention of movable type and printing presses made the word of God available to those who could read. Many Europeans were struck anew with the teachings of Christ and with the importance of the individual in assisting God's will. Access to the Bible and resentment of the abuses in the Roman Catholic Church brought on the Reformation. From the writings of Martin Luther, John Calvin, and others who protested against the concepts and practices of the Church came Protestant churches. Neither Catholic churchmen nor Catholic kings viewed this splintering of Western Christendom with favor. By the Counter Reformation the priesthood eliminated many of the abuses that had crept into the Catholic Church. Temporal rulers who remained faithful to the Church believed that God sanctioned the use of force against "heretical Protestants," and Protestant rulers fought to protect their subjects from Catholic force.

Thus the sixteenth century was an age of new horizons in economics, government, thought, discovery, religion, and freedom. Time and again men broke with tradition to accept new ideas and better ways of doing things. But, as in any age, the struggle for survival between the old and the new was fierce. Catholics fought Protestants with words and swords, and Protestants responded in kind. Kings sent their armies into battle to defend homelands or to add to their territory. Monarchs attempted to grab the best trade routes for their merchants and the richest lands for their colonists. And on occasion conditions within a country gave ambitious nobles hope of recovering power formerly held by their aristocratic ancestors.

This situation prevailed in France in the middle of the sixteenth century. On the death of Francis I in 1547 the throne passed to his son, Henry II, who worked throughout his twelve-year reign to stamp out Protestantism in France. Although supported by his wife, the Florentine Princess Catherine de Medici, Henry's persecution failed to rid France of the "heretics." The writings of French-born John Calvin drew thousands of Frenchmen into the new church; French students studied at the feet of their exiled leader in Switzerland and returned home as missionaries. Notwithstanding the danger involved, the Protestants grew in number, especially among the artisan class in urban communities, until the Huguenots, the name applied to French followers of Calvin, controlled a number of cities in France. In 1559 the Huguenots held their first national synod and their church was in fact an established institution.

That same year Henry II died and was succeeded by his sixteen-year-old son, the physically weak and mentally retarded Francis II. The Duke of Guise and his younger brother, Cardinal Lorraine, seized power and ruled in the name of their incapable monarch. Since they were ardent, intolerant Catholics, they continued Henry's policy of persecuting the Protestants. The princes of the House of Bourbon, "King Anthony" and his younger brother, the Prince of Condé, seized every opportunity to oppose the Catholic nobles. The persecuted Huguenots hated the Duke of Guise and threw their support to the Bourbons. In March, 1560, the latter planned an uprising, but the Guises, forewarned, pounced upon and soundly defeated their political and religious antagonists.

But the victory was fleeting. In December, 1560, Francis died and his mother acted quickly to assume the regency and rule in the name of her ten-year-old son, Charles IX. Perhaps Catherine was primarily a mother trying to preserve the throne of France for her child. Realizing the precariousness of her position, she attempted to win the support of both the Catholic and Huguenot parties. She not only stopped the persecution of the Huguenots but also gave them a limited right to worship as they pleased. These concessions embittered the Catholics, while the unsatisfied Huguenots demanded complete freedom for their form of worship. The passion of religious fanatics on both sides of the controversy foretold failure for Catherine's policy of moderation.

In 1562 some of the escort of the Duke of Guise happened upon a group of Huguenots assembled for worship in a large barn at Vassy. Sharp words led to violence. When Guise rode away, after some efforts by him to stop the fray, thirty Protestants lay dead and almost two hundred wounded. The Duke did not disavow his men's deed, and he was given a hero's welcome by Catholic Paris. Catherine admitted that she lacked power to punish him for the Massacre of Vassy, and the Bourbons sought vengeance in battle. Thus began a series of religious wars and intermittent peace settlements that would continue until 1598.

More and more, in the 1560's, the real leadership of the Huguenots was vested in Gaspard de Coligny, the worthy and gifted Admiral of France, who got along well with Catherine for almost a decade. Admiral Coligny was a convinced, sincere Huguenot but also a patriotic Frenchman. He belonged to the great noble family of Châtillon and, through his mother, was kinsman to the still greater Montmorency family. Although he gained the post of Admiral of France without going to sea, this purely honorary title belonged to a man whose solid character and outstanding ability placed him far above the factious leaders of his time.

Into this age of new horizons René de Laudonnière was born, and his destiny led him to become an active participant both in the religious wars and in the overseas expansion of France.

# II

# *"The Dog" Violates the Law of Kingdoms and Christianity*

ENE de Goulaine de Laudonnière came from a distinguished family which, according to French custom, sometimes used more than one name for its surname, usually a place name added to a family name; in this instance, "Goulaine" and "Laudonnière." These names were often used jointly by the family, as the American Du Pont family of French extraction at times adds "de Nemours." The Goulaines were long-time rulers in Brittany.[3] From about 1440 they held manorial lands in an area designated as Laudonnière in the Province of Poitou.[4]

The exact date of René de Laudonnière's birth is unknown; however, the two portraits of him, presumably painted during his lifetime, indicate that he was born in 1529. Perhaps his birthplace was Dieppe. The few records relating to his activities in the 1550's refer to him as a citizen of that city. His adherence to the Protestant faith also supports the contention that Dieppe was the place of his birth or rearing, for it was a stronghold of the Huguenots. Whether his parents were members of the new faith or he became a convert to it from Catholicism was not recorded or the record has been lost. In all probability he grew up a member of the persecuted sect. Whatever the ambitions of his youth, he was attracted to the sea and by the discoveries of earlier and contemporary explorers.

Laudonnière's contemporary, and antagonist in Florida, Pedro Menéndez de Avilés, reported that the Frenchman was a relative of Admiral Coligny.[5] The Spanish leader also claimed that Laudonnière once served as the administrative assistant of Coligny. Both references indicate the close tie of Laudonnière with the Bourbon and Huguenot faction of France.

7

A 16th century map of Brittany, showing Lodun, the seat of the Laudon-nière family, and Dieppe, the home town of René de Laudonnière. His port of embarkation for America, Havre-de-Grâce, was at the location named on the map as "S. Salua."

Most of what is known of him prior to 1562 is found in the correspondence of 1561 between the Court of France and Sebastien de l'Aubespine, Bishop of Limoges and French Ambassador to Spain.[6] According to this correspondence, a ship flying the royal flag of Charles IX and named *Le Chien*, or *The Dog*, was seized off the waters of Catalonia by Aparceo de Uquarte, lieutenant of Juan de Mendoça, captain of the Spanish galleys. The seizure was made on the pretext that *The Dog* was carrying a cargo to Algeria "contre la loi des Royaumes et de la Chrétienté," or against the law of Kingdoms and Christianity. The captain of *Le Chien* was Laudonnière.

His vessel was loaded with ten kegs of olive oil, cloth of wool and damask, cotton and yarn, spices, wine, and dried codfish. While these were normal commodities for a merchant ship, there were in the cargo seventy hundredweight of lead, some iron, and "above all" fifty oars or tent frames "which the Spanish considered contraband of war." The Spanish officials had previously accused the French of furnishing Algeria with munitions against "la loi universelle de la Chrétienté contre ceul qui portent armes aux infidels." Clearly the Spanish believed that certain of the supplies aboard *The Dog* violated the universal law of Christianity against providing arms to pagans.

*The Dog* was taken by the viceroy of Catalonia, its artillery brought ashore, and all of its merchandise was consigned to the proper agents, except the contraband which was officially confiscated. The officers and crew of *The Dog* were freed, including "Captain Diepa," or Laudonnière, as the captain of the vessel was alternatively designated in the documents. He was also referred to as "the gentleman of the Admiral," or Admiral Gaspard de Coligny's lieutenant. Captain Diepa undoubtedly alluded to *The Dog's* home port and Laudonnière's residence, Dieppe, France. The nautical instruments—three astrolabes, two cross-staffs for elevation studies, declination rules, and several charts—used on *The Dog* were characteristic of the period.

The Spanish officials made a detailed list of Laudonnière's personal property aboard *The Dog*. His belongings included some rather fancy clothes, fancy at least by modern seagoing standards.

In his wardrobe were a short coat of black taffeta, a tooled-leather collar from Morocco, a doublet of white taffeta decorated with crimson silk, a gray cloak with a velvet border two feet in width, and a pair of black woolen cloth shoes trimmed with velvet. Also listed was armor for the upper body (*cuirassine*) and armor for the head and face (*bourguignottes*).

By far the most interesting of Laudonnière's possessions was a rare nautical clock in a gold case lined with crimson velvet. The clock was listed at such a high valuation that it could hardly have been the usual hourglass timekeeper. It must have been an extremely rare "ancestor" of a modern clock. Also itemized were a hunting gun, a silver whistle, a sword, and a book of his personally owned nautical charts. Among his other possessions were some pieces of cloth which he may have intended for his wife, a friendly girl, or even for the kind little old lady who may have lived at the end of his street in Dieppe. Or, perhaps, these materials were to be exchanged for the goods of Algerian natives. In addition, Laudonnière had some Alexandrian linen, some crimson damask, scarlet cloth, and other damask the color of "peach blossoms."

The only other evidence of Laudonnière's work prior to 1562 comes from his writing. In describing his 1564 expedition to Florida he stated: "My Lord Admiral [Coligny] being well informed of the faithful service which I had done as well unto his Majesty Charles IX as to his predecessors, Kings of France, advised the King how able I was to do him service in this voyage." Certainly Laudonnière was active in the nautical service of Charles IX and his predecessors, Francis II and Henry II. The captain from Dieppe was eighteen when Francis I died, but in an era when youths went to sea in their teen-age years, Laudonnière may have started his career during the reign of Francis I.

Certainly before he had reached his thirty-third year, he was an experienced commander and one of the outstanding sea captains of France. His financial success is attested to by the value of his personal possessions on his ship, *The Dog*. By 1562 France was ready to participate in the benefits to be derived from the Age of Discovery, and Laudonnière was also prepared to contribute the leadership needed by his country. He was representative of those impatient members of the human race who were to use the New World in their quest for opportunity and freedom. A capable seaman and an ardent advocate of the reformed religion, he exemplified the twin developments of his era: science and religion.

# III

# *Exploring Florida with Ribault*

Y 1562 Spain was well established in the New World. From her silver and gold mines in Mexico and Peru came precious metals to enrich her and to capture the imagination of the rulers of other European countries. Except for Spain, only Portugal, with Brazil in South America and trading colonies in the Orient, was reaping substantial benefits from overseas enterprises. The Netherlands were fighting mighty Spain for independence, England was moving toward stability under Queen Elizabeth, and France was torn by civil war. Audacious English sea raiders were capturing treasure-laden Spanish galleons, and the French were planning to settle on territory claimed by Spain.

Other than Mexico, the vast continent of North America was only touched by Spain. In 1513 Ponce de León had discovered and named Florida. In the following years Pánfilo de Narváez, Hernando de Soto, and other Spanish conquistadors explored the land. In 1559 a large colonization expedition sailed from Vera Cruz to Pensacola where for two years the Spaniards vainly attempted to establish a permanent settlement. This failure made Philip II of Spain issue a decree[7] prohibiting additional exploration of and settlement in Florida, the name applied by Spain to all of North America lying north of the Rio Grande and the Gulf of Mexico. The King of Spain realized the geographic value of Florida, but too many of his subjects had died in futile efforts to find fortunes or found colonies in the wilderness.

The French people yearned for a bright spot in the sunlight of national colonial expansion. The nation was proud of her navigators who had explored the eastern coasts of North America during the reign of Francis I. These discoveries by Frenchmen gave

12

France claim to North America—a claim equally as good if not more valid than that of Spain. But it had been almost thirty years since the French colors had flown over ships sailing those shores on exploring expeditions. Courageous French fishermen did cross the ocean to catch codfish, but the French pride and economy needed settlements in the New World.

Catherine de Medici heartily endorsed the idea of a French overseas empire. Colonies offered her nation opportunity for increasing her commerce, finding precious metals, and securing valuable lands. Successful colonization would strengthen the throne of Catherine's son Charles IX, and weaken the political position of the ambitious Duke of Guise and the equally grasping Bourbons. The religious controversy in France was a significant motive for French expansion. Admiral Coligny suggested that settlements would provide a haven for the Huguenots,[8] and this idea appealed to Catherine who was then attempting a moderate policy to ease religious conflict. Royal support for colonial enterprise particularly designed for Protestants would certainly win some support from Huguenot leaders. A settlement was attempted along the northeastern shore of South America in 1555, but French attention turned more and more to North America, the lands France claimed by reason of the discoveries of Verrazano and Cartier and as yet unsettled by nationals of any European country.

Perhaps the patriotic Coligny selected Florida as the place for settlement in 1562 because of its nearness to Spanish possessions. Warships based at a port in peninsular Florida would be in easy striking distance of Spain's important Havana settlement in Cuba. Furthermore, the Spanish treasure fleet sailing home from Portobelo, Panama, followed the Bahama Channel along the eastern coast of Florida. The possibilities for raiding Spain's commerce staggered the imagination. But if this was a major objective, Coligny bypassed it to emphasize others—permanent settlement, commerce, and a place for Huguenots to worship free from restrictions.

To lead the expedition Coligny chose Jean Ribault of Dieppe, the most famous of all France's outstanding sea captains. Undoubtedly the Admiral was also instrumental in appointing Laudonnière second in command, but surely Ribault approved of the appointment. At Havre-de-Grâce these leaders began outfitting ships and recruiting sailors and colonists.

There was a multiplicity of reasons for individuals signing up for the perilous voyage and facing hardships in a strange land. Besides their nationalistic and patriotic impulses, they individually sought a haven of freedom, a chance for a new life, adventure, the rewards from discovery of gold and silver, and had an infinite variety of other grounds for leaving their homeland. A contemporary description[9] of one young colonist in 1565 "comme jeune homme curieux de voir le monde," or as a young man wishing to see the world, may have fitted many of the recruits. Most of them were French Protestants, but some were French Catholics, and others were of various nationalities. Still others were touched by anticlericalism and were rebels against all religious formality and especially against religious zealots. Although the overwhelming majority were working-class men, there were several individuals of the nobility and numbers of pardoned criminals. Thus a motley collection of sailors and colonists were signed by Ribault and Laudonnière for the expedition.

On February 18, 1562, they sailed from Havre-de-Grâce in three ships and followed a circuitous route to avoid meeting Spanish men-of-war. Ribault sighted the east coast of Florida and on May 1 entered the mouth of a majestic river which he named the River of May (now the St. Johns). There he landed and prayers were sent heavenward in thanksgiving for a safe voyage. These Frenchmen were the first people to come to an area, now a part of the United States, seeking freedom of religion, and their prayers were the first ever offered on our shores by men searching for fulfillment of their ideals.

Ribault erected a column on the south bank of the river to claim the land for France and to give promise of eventual return and settlement. Before leaving the river valley, the Frenchmen inspected a seventy-foot bluff (now called St. Johns Bluff) as a possible site for a colony, and made friends with the Indians. Then they sailed out into the Atlantic Ocean and northward to present-day South Carolina. At what is now known as Parris Island they set another monument to mark the northern limit of lands claimed by their discovery. Thirty men volunteered, or were ordered, to remain as colonists and Charlesfort, named to honor Charles IX, was built for their protection. Then Ribault and his other men sailed back to France.

His intention was to gather additional colonists and load ships with supplies for a return trip to insure the permanency of the Charlesfort settlement. But he found France in the midst of religious and civil war. Unable to secure support in France, he traveled to England and appealed to Queen Elizabeth. Although the shrewd Queen doubted Ribault's interest in advancing English fortunes, she aided him in collecting supplies and outfitting ships. Changing her mind after she had been convinced that he remained a patriotic Frenchman, she had him imprisoned. Ribault productively spent his time in England writing an account of his voyage to Florida and gave his justification for French and English claims to lands in the New World.[10]

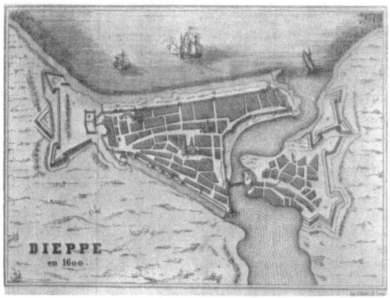

Le Sieur Tassin, *Les Plans et profils de toutes les principales villes* (Paris, Cramoisy, 1634), p. 156

View of 16th Century Dieppe, home town of René de Laudonnière and Jean Ribault.

And what was Laudonnière doing during this period? On returning to Dieppe in 1562, he and Ribault found their city invested by the Catholic forces of the Duke of Guise. Undoubtedly Laudonnière joined in the unsuccessful defense of that city. When it fell, Ribault escaped to England but Laudonnière evidently remained in his home town. The war between the Catholic and Huguenot parties continued with all its fury and cruelty. In 1563 the Duke of Guise was assassinated, and in the same year the Treaty of Amboise ended the first of the wars between the Catholics and the Huguenots. Once more Admiral Coligny had the ear of Queen Mother Catherine, and he was determined to continue the colonization project started in 1562.

Most of the Frenchmen left at Charlesfort returned to France under grim circumstances. Left among the Indians of the coast, the colonists at first found the natives friendly; but as the Europeans demanded more and more of the Indians' meager supplies of corn, the independent natives turned against the European interlopers. The lack of food, the discouragement, and finally the hopelessness of their situation created discord. One man named Larcher was banished from the fort; the other men turned on their leader and executed him. They proceeded to build a ship, stock it with all available supplies, and sail for home.

*They set out to sea on the first good wind. The calms and erratic gusts soon held them captive and the fresh water and victuals gave out. Since in three weeks they had advanced only 25 leagues they were restricted to eating not more than twelve grains by weight of corn meal per man per day. But even this gave out, and they devoured their shoes, leather collars, straps, and dried animal skins. Those who tried the sea water suffered with swollen throats and scorched their guts with strange torments. So, others drank their own urine. . . . They remained without food or drink for three days. Finally, it was suggested that it would be wiser that one die rather than all of them. The lot fell on the banished Larcher. He was killed and his flesh was equally divided among them. Then they drank his warm blood.[11]*

The survivors were eventually picked up by a British ship. So ended the first attempt at settlement by Frenchmen in the territory called Florida by Spain and New France by France.

# IV

# *Threshold of Freedom—America's Beginning*

IBAULT'S expedition of 1562 was more of an exploring than a colonizing venture. In 1564 Coligny was determined to have Frenchmen establish a permanent settlement somewhere in Florida. Since Ribault was imprisoned in England, the Admiral naturally turned to René de Laudonnière, who had been second in command on the 1562 voyage. Because of his "prudence and blameless life," the "very religious" Laudonnière was authorized to choose "brave, upright and intelligent men" for the colonial enterprise.

In March and April, 1564, the commander outfitted vessels and selected sailors, soldiers, and colonists. For his flagship he chose the *Isabel of Honfleur,* a 300-ton galleon originally built for naval-duty, and armed her with ten or twelve heavy guns. The *Petit Breton* of 120 or 200 tons, and the 80-ton *Falcon* were also fitted with guns. Into their holds went munitions: cannon for a fort in the New World, "ammunition, pikes, arquebuses, armor, gunpowder, bullets, explosive devices, and other things." Supplies for colonists included agricultural equipment, animals, foodstuffs, millstones for grinding grain, and seed. To these essentials of settlement were added the belongings of individual colonists—clothing, religious books, and other personal items.

The personnel of this expedition were more diverse than those of the previous one. Some of the leading families of France were represented; and some of the worst as well as some of the best elements of French society. Gentlemen appeared in gilded armor and brightly colored clothes, laborers were dressed in plain garments, and artisans wore good, durable clothing. The overwhelming

majority were Huguenots, but there were Catholics, agnostics, and
perhaps "infidels." These latter came from Africa,[12] apparently free
men and not slaves. The French desire for permanency in settlement was illustrated by the inclusion of women, of whom at least
four had husbands. Certainly the strong motivation of many Huguenots was their desire for religious freedom. They and their companions were seeking opportunity and freedom in a distant land
where they could live under the French flag.

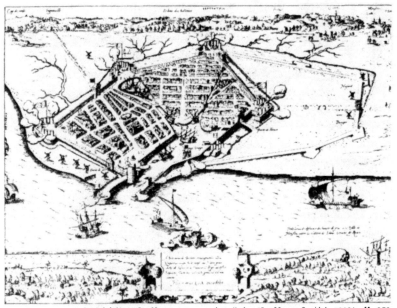

J. Adeleline, *Le Havre a travers les siècles* (Le Havre Société, 1909), II, 270

View of 16th century (1563) Havre-de-Grâce, whence Laudonnière departed
for America in 1564.

On April 22 the three ships with their three hundred people
aboard sailed southwest from Havre-de-Grâce into the Atlantic.
They passed the Canary Islands, moved on across the wide ocean
into the Caribbean Sea, and stopped briefly at Santo Domingo.
Then Laudonnière headed them toward Florida, and he sighted the
River of May on June 24, 1564. The following day he explored the
territory along the south bank of the river which Ribault had described as "the fairest, frutefullest and pleasantest of all the

worlde." The "sight of the faire medows," he had added, "is a pleasure not able to be expresed with tongue." Laudonnière thought "the place was so pleasant that melancholias would be forced to change their nature" as they viewed it.

The site selected for settlement was a beautifully wooded area, now St. Johns Bluff, located on the south side of the river about ten miles east of the central business section of present-day Jacksonville, Florida. The choice of this section was made for several reasons. Laudonnière remembered it favorably from the 1562 expedition. The bluff commanded the river, the adjacent land was fertile, and the Indians received the Frenchmen in friendship. The fields of corn, the native grapes and other fruits, and the products of the woods indicated the land's ability to sustain human life. Not only was the area defensible but also its closeness to the Atlantic Ocean afforded easy access for additional colonists and supplies from France, and the broad, languid St. Johns River was a waterway into the interior where gold and silver might be found.

The colonists named their settlement La Caroline to honor their King Charles. On June 30 the sounding of trumpets called them together in assembly to give thanks to God for their successful voyage and the auspicious beginning of the colony. They sang a psalm of thanksgiving and asked God's blessing for "our enterprise that all might turn to His glory."

But the French were realists. They immediately began constructing a fort which they called Fort Caroline, and this name rather than La Caroline gradually became the designated one for their settlement. Aided by the friendly Indians, they built a triangular fortification on the flat land at the river side west of the bluff. To these lowlands they gave the name of the Vale of Laudonnière. The triangular fort was constructed of "timber and faggots" and earthen banks. Moats were dug on its two sides away from the river and an impressive gate was constructed and decorated with the arms of France and their patron, Admiral Coligny. Inside the fort buildings housed the munitions. Some houses were erected within the fortification, but many others were built outside its protective walls of timber and sand. Sentinels were stationed by the fort and on the nearby St. Johns Bluff to watch for and protect the

André Thevet, *Cosmographie Universelle* (Paris, 1575)

A 16th century illustration of bison in Florida.

settlers from surprise attack from unfriendly Indians or Spanish
soldiers. In their haste to explore, find precious metals, or do other
interesting things, the French did not entirely complete their fort's
walls by buttressing them with sturdy logs.

After getting his settlement started, Laudonnière sped the two
larger ships back to France with his request for additional supplies
and 500 more colonists. The colonists then began to make their
new homes habitable. Beds were framed within houses or ham-
mocks strung between trees, according to the preference of individuals. Some artisans used the local clay to make crude brick or
selected rock for building material. It was not long before a flour
mill, a bakery, and a blacksmith shop were in being. Among the
settlers were carpenters, blacksmiths, tailors,. barbers, shoemakers,
and brewers in addition to a crossbow maker, a physician, an as-

tronomer, an artist, mechanics, and ordnance men. At first there was no ordained preacher and religious services were conducted by dedicated laymen. A large bell was rung to call the colonists to worship, and religious services were conducted every afternoon. Sometime later a minister arrived on a ship bearing supplies and settlers from France.

As a whole these French people were not long-faced zealots. They found pleasure in primitive Florida in earthly pursuits as well as in religious services. The native grapes gave them the raw material for wine. One colonist wrote: "We hope to make some wine soon, which will be just fine." Records indicate the wine-making was a success, for twenty barrels were produced at one time. The colonists were intrigued by tobacco and quickly began to smoke it. In addition they enjoyed music by a fiddler, a spinet player, drummers, trumpeters, and fifers. Long after Fort Caroline had become history, the Indians of the region sang songs that they had learned from the light-hearted French colonists. Cards brought from France were used by the idle to pass time in a pleasant fashion. Nature's provision for continuation of the species could not be denied. It is recorded that eight or more children were born at Fort Caroline.[13] Unfortunately the names of the first children born of Europeans in what eventually became a part of the United States were not recorded, but certainly their births antedated that of Virginia Dare by more than two decades.

Too many of the Frenchmen played while supplies of food brought from France dwindled away. The three small ships and the space required for passengers and essential defensive weapons left only limited space for foodstuffs. The wild fields and forests and the neighborhood Indian farmers produced scant food for the many mouths of the settlers. Wild game, even bison,[14] were present but not in great numbers. While awaiting the promised supplies from France, the settlers at Fort Caroline made deep inroads into their store of food.

From the vantage point of four hundred years it is easy to criticize Laudonnière for failing to put his men to work clearing land and planting crops. In reality the Florida growing season was too advanced for successful cultivation. Furthermore, the friendliness of the Indians and the pleasant sight of their cornfields gave the colonists a false sense of security. They failed to realize that Indian agriculture produced little more than enough to feed the native inhabitants. Two hundred extra consumers could and quickly did use the surplus food of nearby tribes. Then, too, Laudonnière expected a flow of colonists and supplies from France. Later in 1564 a Captain Bourdet arrived from France with settlers and food, but the mother country was niggardly in supplying her infant colony. The men at Fort Caroline were interested in the new land and naturally turned to exploring its terrain and resources.

Perhaps the fundamental reason for the neglect of agriculture lay in one of the purposes for founding the colony. French leaders were anxious to find gold and silver, trade with the natives, and increase the commerce of France. Laudonnière sought diligently to develop resources of wealth for his country; particularly, substantial efforts were made to find gold and he insisted that all precious metals should be held for the French government. Forty-three years later the English colonists were to waste valuable time in digging for gold (which turned out to be iron pyrites) and shipping it back to England. The tremendous amount of silver and gold being obtained by Spain made other Europeans eager to search for quick wealth rather than immediately developing a substantial and enduring agricultural program.

The French colonists relied upon the promises made at the beginning of their expedition—that their settlement would be maintained by supplies from France. Since these promises were not kept to any appreciable degree, the Fort Caroline settlers had to rely heavily upon the Indians. The natives were looked to both for food and for trade.

On their first arrival at St. Johns Bluff, Laudonnière with a detachment of twelve soldiers reconnoitered the land. Three Indian chiefs with more than 400 of their tribesmen met them and made signs of friendship. The Indians who had learned to hate and fear the Spaniards welcomed the French. It also appeared that the natives not only recalled the visit of Ribault but had made a god of him, and the column he had erected had become their idol. They quickly made a request for help in fighting a neighboring tribe that was a three-days journey away, but not wanting to become involved in warfare between the natives, Laudonnière put the chiefs off with vague and evasive promises. Despite later difficulties, the French leader managed to retain the friendship and help of Chief Saturiba and of many other Indian leaders who probably admired his shrewdness, a quality which they coveted in themselves.

But Laudonnière's men found no more than trinkets of gold and silver in possession of the Indians living near Fort Caroline. To fulfill his obligation to his superiors at home, he sent an expedition up the St. Johns to search for the valuable metals. The party led by a Mr. d'Antigny and a Captain Vasseur went about sixty leagues up the river, but found the Indians shy and fearful. To entice the Indians, some attractive goods were left in barges at the water's edge, the French withdrew a considerable distance, and the suspicious but curious natives gradually went to see what their visitors had left. Reassured, they made friendly signs and took the French to their village for a "ceremonious welcome." The French returned to Fort Caroline with reports of gold and silver mines within the Indian territory.

Despite these pleasant prospects Laudonnière discovered in the immediate area neither productive mines nor an abundance of gold and silver jewelry. Some gold and silver bartered with the Indians and the lure of mines in the "Apalatcy" mountains made him consider moving the colony nearer the metal deposits in what is now northern Georgia and North Carolina.[15] The colonists, however, were forever searching for sources of immediate wealth and at times their activities resulted in their capture by unfriendly Indians.

The French generally found the natives "good people" with pleasant dispositions. Although they frequently waged war and either killed or enslaved their luckless captives, they were not cannibalistic. The land produced good crops of corn, the forests abounded in deer and other game, and the waters teemed with fish. Walnuts, chestnuts, and "many good grapes, sweet and plump" were sources of food and wine. The Europeans were amazed at the "endless variety of trees, cedars, pines, swamp oaks, and live oaks producing acorns which the Indians eat. . . . " The timber proved

Placer mining for gold by Indians in "Apalatcy" mountains in 1564-65. One of Le Moyne's series of America's first landscapes and action drawings.

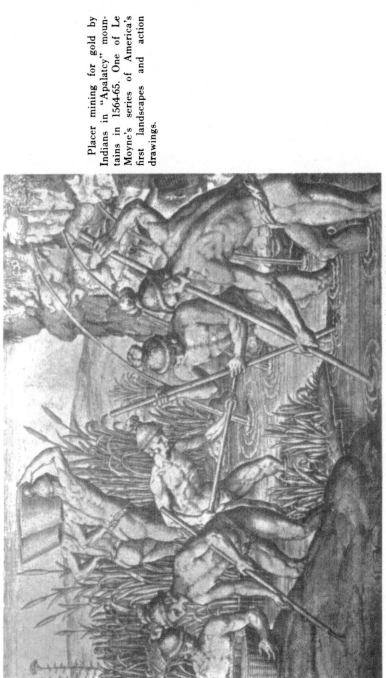

*Brevis Narratio* (Frankfort, de Bry, 1591)

to be excellent in quality and French artisans built "a very good 18-bench galley boat" from some of it. They were surprised to find no domestic animals and concluded that the Indians were a lazy people.

The Indians did supply the French with some products which could have become the basis for trade with the mother country. Metals, hides, pearls, and various plants were sent back to France. One plant used by the Indians for medicinal purposes was named "sassafras" by the colonists, and Laudonnière shipped samples of its roots to the king with the hope that it would become a source of medicine and commerce. Tobacco, which had been introduced into France by Jean Nicot, the French ambassador in Portugal, was found and considered a potentially valuable medicinal plant. The word "nicotine" came from Nicot's name.

From those colonists who occupied themselves in trading with the Indians came an interesting account of Pierre Gambré. This French youth established himself as a businessman and trader on an island in the St. Johns, probably the land now known as Fleming's Island. Before long he prospered, married the daughter of an Indian chief, and rose to second in command with the Indians. After living with the Indians for about a year, he decided to visit Fort Caroline. On the trip he was murdered by an Indian. The murderer was apparently motivated by resentment from a previous dispute with Gambré and desire to obtain the riches which the French boy had acquired through his business dealings with the Indians.[16]

Keeping order among colonists who sought wealth by trade or discovery of gold was not an easy task. Most of them were not accustomed to military discipline, but the circumstances of their living in lands of a primitive people who had not invited them required a community discipline not unlike military service in some respects. Because some colonists chafed under this form of discipline, Laudonnière later wrote:

*It is very hard, yea utterly impossible, that in governing a company of men gathered out of divers places and sundry Nations, and namely such as we know them to be in our warres, it is, I say, impossible, but there will be always some of evil conditions and*

*hard to be ruled, which easily conceive an hatred against him,*
*which by his admonitions and light connections endevoureth to re-*
*duce them to the discipline of warre. For they seek nothing else,*
*but for a small occasion grounded on a light pretext to sound unto*
*the eares of great Lords that which mischievously they have con-*
*trived against those, whose execution of justice is odious unto*
*them.* [17]

One problem in the Florida wilderness was sex. With the relatively few available French women already claimed by husbands,
the few remaining men sought companionship and love from Indian maidens. Neither the unattached native girls nor their fathers
opposed matches between an Indian maiden and a Frenchman. The
Indians probably considered living together conclusive evidence
of marriage, but without a formal ceremony most Europeans believed themselves participating in temporary affairs of convenience.
Laudonnière experienced considerable difficulty with the "Moors"
and with paroled criminals. One man, an interpreter, was "married to a native woman whom he did not wish to leave nor yet acknowledge for his wife." Laudionnière ruled against liaisons with
the Indian women "unless they were joined together in good and
lawful marriage, and that they should abandon their wicked ways
on pain of death. . . . " Some of the men, particularly the Moors,
lived lustily "without God, without faith, without law," and found
it difficult "to leave their mistresses and lead a better life, to live
as decent people and in the company of Christians."[18]

This moralistic order of Laudonnière conflicts with the accusations made by his detractors. According to his critics he brought a
mistress on the voyage and lived with her at Fort Caroline. Laudonnière denied the charge.

*The woman was a poore chambermayd [he wrote], which I*
*had taken up in an Inne, to oversee my household business, to look*
*to an infinite sort of divers beasts, as sheepe and poultrie which I*
*carried with me to store the country withall: that it was not meete*
*to put a man to attend this business: likewise, considering the*
*length of the time that I was to abide there, mee thought it should*
*not offend anybody to take a woman with me, as well to help my*
*soldiers in their sicknesses, as in mine owne, whereunto I fell after-*
*wards.*

If indeed Laudonnière had a mistress, his act would not have been unusual among Frenchmen of the sixteenth century. The weight of evidence, however, supports his contention that she was a poor chambermaid brought to America to be his housekeeper, shepherdess, and practical nurse. His giving opportunity to the poor girl was in keeping with his compassionate character and was consistent with his general attitude toward people in trouble. He was both sympathetic and generous to a Santo Domingo Indian whom the Spaniards had emasculated. When the food supply at Fort Caroline became depleted, the commander placed himself on the same strict ration that applied to the other colonists. For a time he kept a pet falcon, one that he had saved from a snake in Florida, but he freed it rather than retain it for his personal pleasure when the supply of food became inadequate at the fort. It is also significant that none of the people at Caroline referred to the girl as Laudonnière's mistress—to them she was his housekeeper and nothing more. Only the malcontents who returned to France accused their former commander of indiscretion. After the destruction of Fort Caroline the "poore chambermayd" was sent back to France where she won a husband and raised a large family.

The sincerity of Laudonnière's religious faith forces the historian to question a misalliance. Followers of Calvin were rather strict in their moral life. While some Huguenot men of higher French society had mistresses, many of them adhered to a puritanical moral code in the practice of their reformed religion. Certainly Laudonnière emphasized religious observation at Fort Caroline. At first there was no ordained minister for the settlers and religious services were conducted by laymen. The ringing tones of a large bell called the people to worship, usually every afternoon. Shortly after establishing Fort Caroline, indignation was "felt by many who professed the desire of living according to the doctrine of the reformed gospel, for the reason that they found themselves without a minister of God's word."[19] This deficiency was overcome by the arrival of a preacher, who probably came with the reinforcement expedition of Captain Bourdet later in 1564. When the Spaniards defeated the French at Fort Caroline the next year, these Catholics took pride in the number of "heretical Bibles" and other religious books found and burned. Services at the settlement and the missionary work of the Huguenots among the Indians prove the strong religious feelings of many of the colonists. Under these circumstances it is doubtful that Laudonnière set a bad example for his followers.

There is, however, no question about his having serious difficulty as a leader of the colony. Jacques Le Moyne de Morgues, the artist who joined the colonial venture for the primary purpose of making maps and painting pictures, characterized Laudonnière as a man "of varied abilities, though experienced not so much in military as in naval affairs." The artist believed Laudonnière too easily influenced by some of the colonists, but this criticism must be considered along with that of other settlers who accused their leader of being too firm. "It is necessary for a Governor," Laudonnière wrote, "to make himselfe knowen and obeyed, for feare least every body would become a master." In defending himself after returning to France, he made comments which deserve repeating:

*We see how the good name of the most honest is oftentimes assayled by such, as having no meanes to win themselves credit by vertuous and laudable endevours, thinke by debasing of other mens vertues to augment the feeble force of their faint courages, which neverthelesse is one of the most notable dangers, which may happen in a commonwealth, and chiefly among men of warre which are placed in government.*

Perhaps the most striking illustration of his firmness was his insistence that none of the 100 chickens possessed by the colony be killed for food, and this was at a time when the bones of many colonists were showing through their skins because of hunger. He held steadfast to his purpose and plan, namely, the permanency of the colony, and retaining sufficient poultry for the future needs was essential. Le Moyne claimed that some colonists died of starvation. Laudonnière admitted that men picked up fishbones from the floor and ate them to sustain life. Under these trying circumstances he firmly gave the future priority over the present.

Malcontents found their leader inadequate in his Indian policy. Some of them criticized him for not joining the local Indians in making war on their enemies, while others accused him of arousing native anger by aggressiveness. Admittedly he was unwilling to use the superior weapons of France in aiding one Indian tribe against another and embroiling the colonists in war. He told his friend and main Indian benefactor, Chief Saturiba, that the French could not give help once promised to Saturiba for an expedition against Chief Outina because "for his [Saturiba's] amitie I would not purchase the enmitie of the other." Laudonnière exerted every effort to trade mirrors, beads, knives, and hatchets for Indian corn to feed the colonists and for other commodities to establish trade between America and France.

He was not above playing on the Indians' superstitions, however, and meeting their craftiness with a craftiness of his own. Once the Indians watched 500 acres of their meadows being consumed by a fire started by lightning, but they believed the burning had been caused by French guns. Capitalizing on the Indians' ignorance of gunpowder, Laudonnière told their chief "that I was content to shoote the halfe way to make him knowe my force; assuring him furthermore, that on condition that he would continue in his good affection, no more ordinance should be discharged against him hereafter."

Three points that offset the criticism of Laudonnière in his crafty dealings with the Indians must be considered. First, his attitude toward alliances and the keeping of promises was cut from the same pattern as that used by his king and most of the other monarchs of the sixteenth century. Secondly, the Indians were well known to be highly deceptive themselves, and arrangements for future action under such circumstances were probably taken with a grain of salt by all participants. Thirdly, the precarious existence of the colony required that he enforce rigid, unpleasant measures which might not have been necessary in a thriving prosperous settlement. It is true that he led an expedition to capture an Indian chief and held him as hostage until tribesmen delivered foodstuffs to the colonists, but this event took place during the "starving time" at Fort Caroline and after mutineers had imprisoned Laudonnière and had considered murdering him. Such action during these trying times is understandable. When he allowed his followers to participate in Indian warfare, he did so under duress and not by choice.

Discontent in the colony stemmed from many causes. The riches expected from gold, silver, and pearls did not materialize. French leaders failed to send the supplies they had promised in support of the infant colony. The Indian tribes produced comparatively little in agricultural surplus and when the colonists' need for corn and other staple foods had seriously depleted the Indians' stores, their friendship was transformed into enmity. The grasping and always hungry Frenchmen appeared selfish and unreliable to a primitive people. Although sixteenth century Frenchmen enjoyed few of the luxuries of twentieth century society, the colonists found the privations of colonial life unbearable compared to their comforts at home. Frustrated, disappointed, and rebellious, some of the colonists blamed their woes on Laudonnière; others sought riches in attacking Spanish commerce. Thirteen of them stole a vessel, plundered the Cuban coast, and were promptly captured by the Spanish. Then in December, 1564, sixty-six others mutinied, seized Laudonnière while he slept, left him in chains, and sailed to Cuban waters. At first they were successful in their forays against Spanish shipping, but off Jamaica a Spanish squadron overcame them. Eventually some of the mutineers were lucky enough to escape from the king's war vessels and return to Fort Caroline. Laudonnière held a trial and as a result several of the rebellious colonists were executed.

There was no denying, however, that Fort Caroline was, in the minds of most of the colonists, a failure. The deficiencies in foodstuffs, the discontent of most of the colonists, and the frequent rebellions against Laudonnière foretold the end of France's colonial experiment in Florida. During the spring and early summer months of 1565, sentinels watched for sails on the horizon, hopeful that underneath them were ships loaded with supplies and settlers to augment their infant colony. Days, weeks, and months passed without the longed-for aid from home. Perhaps reluctantly, Laudonnière agreed that the only possible action was, at least temporarily, to abandon the colony and return to France. Woodsmen felled trees, with axes the logs were hewed into timbers, and carpenters fitted the boards into a ship of sufficient size to withstand the waters of the Atlantic.

Then in August, 1565, hope was revived by the appearance of ships in the St. Johns. At first the watchmen could not determine whether they flew the French or Spanish flag. Everyone was surprised on learning that the vessels were English, the flagship *Jesus* of Sir John Hawkins and other ships, putting into the river for a supply of fresh water. Hawkins had begun his career as a slave trader, supplying the Spanish colonies with labor in exchange for goods. He had quickly found it more profitable to attack Spanish vessels and ports and relieve them of their gold and silver. At this time Spain was the colossus to be attacked by England and France, but the latter countries had no fundamental enmity toward each other.

Circumstances fortuitous for the French had brought Hawkins to the St. Johns. A sailor on one of his vessels declared the water was rationed and every man aboard the ships "was contented to pinch his own bellie, whatsoever happened," but a strong wind had prevented Hawkins from putting in at an inlet lower on the Florida coast to secure fresh water. The English sailors were intrigued by the habits of the Frenchmen at Fort Caroline. One later wrote:

*The Floridians when they travell, have a kinde of herbe dried, who with a cane and an earthen cup in the end, with fire, and the dried herbs put together, doe sucke thorow the cane the smoke thereof, which smoke satisfieth their hunger, and therewith they live four or five dayes without meat or drinke, and this all the Frenchmen used for this purpose: yet do they holde opinion withall, that it causeth water and fleame to void from their stomacks.*[20]

The imagination of the English sailors created monsters in Florida—unicorns and three-headed beasts roaming the woods near Fort Caroline. But Sir John Hawkins was a realist. A ship captured from its Spanish owners needed brass cannon to arm it and the French had cannon. They needed food from the holds of his vessels and he had a ship but lacked the requisite number of sailors to man it. Exchanges were made: the seaworthy vessel and ample food and other supplies for the brass cannon. Hawkins offered to take the French colonists with him and see them across the At-

lantic. Ever the French patriot, Laudonnière declined, for he knew
that abandoning Fort Caroline and accepting the English offer
would give England claim to Florida. He took the proffered ship
and supplies in exchange for most of the cannon at Fort Caroline.

André Thevet, *Cosmographie Universelle* (Paris, 1575)

Illustration of a monstrous beast of Florida described as a rapacious beast
living on the river banks near Fort Caroline. The text indicates that it may be a
common opossum.

After Hawkins had sailed away, a spirit of optimism pervaded
the French colony. Individuals worked with unusual vigor to trans-
fer personal belongings to the recently acquired ship. Water and
food for the voyage back to France were carted aboard. Before the
end of August the Frenchmen awaited a good wind to fill the sails
of their vessels and a high tide to deepen the water at the mouth of
the St. Johns River. Whenever these two conditions occurred simultaneously, they planned on putting to sea and sailing for home.
Unknown to the colonists reinforcements from France and hostile
forces from Spain were approaching the coast of Florida.

# V

## *Succor and Massacre*

HE release of Jean Ribault from prison and his return to France triggered Coligny's plan to send aid to, and make changes at, Fort Caroline. Malcontents had returned from the colony with reports of suffering, mutiny, and poor administration at the fort. Ribault was placed in command of the relief expedition and commissioned to supersede Laudonnière. Seven ships were outfitted and loaded with wheat, biscuit, salted meat, wine, agricultural implements, animals, guns, and ammunition. Able sea captains, including Ribault's son Jacques (also called Loys Ribault), accepted appointments as ship commanders and a total of almost 600 sailors, soldiers, and settlers (men, women, and children) prepared for sailing. While most of these people were French Huguenots, there was a sprinkling of French Catholics and some men from foreign countries. For two weeks the ships lay at anchor awaiting winds to fill their sails and speed them to Florida.

Finally, late in June of 1565, the flotilla began the long voyage to America. More than two months later Ribault sighted the mouth of the St. Johns River. At first, sentinels from Fort Caroline could not determine whether the ships they sighted were French or Spanish, but their apprehension quickly turned to joy. On August 28 the three smallest ships of Ribault's fleet crossed the river bar and proceeded to Fort Caroline. Unable to navigate the shallow water, the four largest ships anchored off the mouth of the river.

The arrival of a new commander with food and additional colonists apparently ensured the permanence of Fort Caroline. Optimism replaced defeatism and all thought of abandoning the colony was erased from the minds of the settlers. At last it appeared that France was fulfilling her promise to support the infant settlement

33

until its courageous inhabitants had time to develop a self-sustain-
ing economy. To many Huguenots the search for religious freedom
seemed to be justified and liberty in a new land secured.

However, that unfortunate caprice of nature which had held
Ribault immobile in France for two weeks dealt the aspirations of
the colonists a mortal blow. Because of the delay, he had only a
week in which to begin his reorganization of the colony before a
Spanish fleet appeared off the St. Johns.

In sixteenth century Europe, just as in the world of the twentieth century, agents of a country investigated and reported the
activities of actual and potential enemy states. Thus Philip II of
Spain learned of the 1562 expedition of Ribault and the colony at
Charlesfort. Before the fate of the unsuccessful attempt to have a
permanent colony at Charlesfort was known, the Spanish monarch
had decreed the destruction of the settlement. By his order the
governor of Cuba instructed Captain Hernando de Manrique de
Rojas to reconnoiter the coast of Florida and exterminate the
French invaders on Spanish territory. The Manrique expedition
sailed from Havana on May 24, 1564, located the "house and fort"
at Charlesfort, burned them, and returned to Havana.

Manrique missed the Fort Caroline expedition, but Spanish
spies at Paris and at ports of France kept Philip II informed of the
French settlement and plans for its reinforcement. The Spanish ambassador at Paris, Don Francisco de Alava, protested again and
again against the French encroachment in Spanish Florida. But
Queen Mother Catherine de Medici repeatedly vowed that her subjects were settling Tierra de las Bretones, a land belonging to
France by right of discovery. To Don Francisco it made no difference whether the territory was called Bretones, the mountains of
Hercules, or New France; it was Spanish Florida and belonged to
Spain. The ambassador appealed to Catherine to withdraw "the
vassals of your king" and threatened to have them removed from
Florida by force unless she ordered them to withdraw.

Philip II was determined to carry out the threat of his ambassador, for Fort Caroline was located at the mouth of the Bahama
Channel through which the Spanish treasure fleets sailed on their
homeward voyage. A powerful fort and supply base for ships of

war at Caroline would endanger the entire trade between Spain and her productive colonies in the New World. The Spanish monarch was convinced that the only reason for the French settlement was to prey on Spanish commerce. For the important task of ridding Florida of the French, Philip selected Pedro Menéndez de Avilés, an ardent and dedicated Catholic, the ablest of Spain's naval commanders and military leaders. Since Spain and France were officially at peace, Menéndez was instructed to seek out any settlers or corsairs in Spanish Florida and drive them out by any means he saw fit to use. After the Menéndez expedition had sailed from Cadiz, Spain, on June 29, 1565, Philip informed Catherine that a royal force was on its way to chastise the French settlers as thieving pirates and perturbers of the public peace. The punitive fleet was delayed by a violent storm, but in spite of repeated blows from nature, a part of it reached Cape Canaveral, Florida, on August 25, 1565.[21] Three days later Menéndez entered a harbor north of the Cape and named it San Augustín for the feast day of St. Augustine. After landing some members of his expedition and depositing supplies on Anastasia Island, he sailed north toward the place where Indians had told him the Frenchmen were settled. On September 4 he sighted the four vessels of Ribault anchored off the mouth of the St. Johns.

The arrival of the Spaniards should not have been a complete surprise to Ribault. In his instructions received before leaving France was a warning of possible Spanish attempts to dislodge French nationals in Florida. His crew was not at battle stations, however, and as the opposing vessels reached hailing distance, Menéndez demanded unconditional surrender. Ribault replied: "I am the Admiral; but I will die first." Not prepared for combat, he cut his anchor cables and his ships outdistanced the lumbering vessels of Menéndez. The Spanish commander gave up the futile chase and returned to the mouth of the St. Johns, but his ships drew too deep a draft to cross the river's bar to attack Fort Caroline. Wisely he sailed south to St. Augustine to establish defenses for his colony.

Shortly thereafter Ribault returned. In conference with Laudonnière, the recently arrived commander planned to take the able-

bodied men at Fort Caroline and attack Menéndez before he could
establish himself at St. Augustine. Laudonnière objected. In his
opinion Fort Caroline ought not to be left practically unmanned
and he thought it unwise to put to sea during the hurricane season. Ribault held out an inducement: after defeating Menéndez he
would allow Laudonnière to retain command at Fort Caroline while
Ribault built another settlement near Caroline. Despite Laudonnière's persistent objections, Ribault sailed south to attack Menéndez.

The aggressive plan of the commander almost succeeded. Near
the mouth of St. Augustine harbor he surprised Menéndez and
barely missed capturing him as well as a sloop and two smaller
boats loaded with men and munitions. But Ribault's ships could
not cross the shallow sandy bar to attack the Spaniards on the
western shore of Anastasia Island or on the mainland. While Ribault waited for a high tide, hurricane winds arrived and swept his
helpless ships southward to their destruction.

For almost two weeks Menéndez directed the establishment of
what became the first permanent community within the territory of
the United States. Then he made a bold move. Knowing that Fort
Caroline must have been left virtually defenseless, he decided to
march overland and attack it. The stormy season and information
obtained from the deposition of Robert Meleneche,[22] one of the
mutinous French pirates of Fort Caroline captured in the Caribbean, convinced Menéndez that an overland expedition started well
to the south had a greater chance of succeeding than one by sea
because of the shallow entrance to the river. Fort Caroline, he had
learned from Meleneche's deposition, was not easily approached on
land along the river bank, which was very marshy. The fort was
built and armed primarily against attack by land—French ships
and the shallow bar protected it on the water side—but the under-
manned fort could be taken from the land side by surprise. Menéndez assembled 500 men, nearly all of his fighting force at St.
Augustine, for the hazardous venture.

Many of his subordinates protested. They feared Ribault
might reappear, kill the people at St. Augustine, and completely destroy the settlement. The force of Menéndez could then be

caught between Laudonnière at Fort Caroline and Ribault at St. Augustine. Menéndez brushed these arguments aside. One Spaniard, Juan de San Vicente, begged off the march by claiming a serious stomach ache and a hurt leg. After Menéndez left, the fearful Spaniard said: "I swear to God that I am expecting the news that all our soldiers have been killed, so that we who remain here may embark on these three ships and go to the Indies, for it is not reasonable that we should all die like beasts."[23]

On September 16, 1565, Menéndez led his men north, guided by a French traitor named Francis Jean. Their route lay through a jungle of underbrush and through swamps and streams. They hacked a pathway and waded hip deep through water. Almost four days were spent in covering the twenty leagues from St. Augustine to the vicinity of Fort Caroline. In the morning darkness of September 20, the force camped at a small pond (which can still be seen today), exhausted, wet, and hungry. About the break of day Menéndez assembled his men at the shores of the pond to decide whether to attack Caroline or return to St. Augustine and leave Florida to the French. Many lieutenants favored retreat, but Menéndez persuaded the majority to concede to the advance on the fort. Mendoza, the chaplain, stated that Menéndez "was a friend of his own opinion." The conference probably served a purpose by bolstering the morale of the soldiers.

The Frenchmen at Fort Caroline were taken by surprise. Although Laudonnière had ordered watchmen to remain on guard, the incessant rain and wind convinced them there could be no danger of an attack by the Spaniards from distant St. Augustine. The few sentinels who remained at their posts were quickly silenced. Most of the people left by Ribault at Caroline were not experienced soldiers, and many of the fighting men lay ill. Laudonnière himself was sick, so sick in fact that he had placed La Vigne in charge of the sentinels and the latter had dismissed most of the guards because of the bad weather and had gone to bed himself.

Menéndez headed the main Spanish attack on the southwest section of the fort. Before the sleeping Frenchmen were fully awake, the Spaniards were inside the fortification and using their pikes and swords with bloody effect. Alerted by the noise of battle, nightshirted Laudonnière jumped from his sickbed to join the fight. The renegade Francis Jean pointed out Captain Laudonnière to the invaders as the Frenchman ran to assist his countrymen who were vainly attempting to prevent more Spaniards from entering the fort. Pikemen drove him back into the court, but he continued to wield his sword until only one companion remained by his side and Spanish flags flew on the ramparts at each corner of Fort Caroline. Then with the fort lost, Laudonnière, unable to stand alone against the aggressors, turned to escape through his house. A tent standing in the way obstructed the Spaniards who pursued him. While they hacked away at its cords, he left the fort by the western breach and ran for the protective cover of trees. Though severely wounded, he assisted others to escape.

In less than an hour the Spaniards won a complete victory, with only one of their men a casualty. Many men and some women and children in the fort were slain in the battle. Some reports of the attack imply that Menéndez was a bit tardy in ordering his men to spare women and children, and state that the bodies of some infants were impaled on pikes stuck in the ground. The rest of the women and children, and some men, including Spanish ship-wrecked sailors to whom the French had given haven, were spared from the wrath of Menéndez. The other men were hanged, according to French accounts, and the inscription placed above their dangling bodies read, "I do this, not as to Frenchmen, but as to Lutherans." Probably as many as 143 Frenchmen were killed or hanged at Fort Caroline.

Victorious Menéndez returned to St. Augustine with his captives and some booty taken at Caroline. The ammunition, clothing, foodstuffs, utensils, agricultural equipment, poultry, and domestic animals were appropriated for Spanish use. The Protestant Bibles and symbols of the Huguenot faith were burned or broken. Before leaving the fort, Menéndez renamed it San Mateo and left many of his men in it. The Spaniard also changed the French River of May to the San Juan River, from which came the name of St. Johns.

Back at St. Augustine, Menéndez wrote a report for his king. He told Philip II, on October 15, 1565,[24] "He who had been Governor and Judge, who called himself Monsieur Laudonnière, a rela-

tive of the Admiral of France who had been his Major Domo fled
to the woods, and a soldier pursuing him gave him a blow with a
pike. We could not see what became of him." More than three
months later Menéndez again mentioned Laudonnière in a letter to
King Philip. "The day that we took the fort," Menéndez wrote, "he
jumped over the wall in his shirt and fled to the mountain wounded
by a pike and we never heard any further news of him. . . . It
seemed to me that he reached the shore before the son of Jean
Ribault got over the bar."[25]

Despite his illness and wound, Laudonnière escaped and, as
has been mentioned, aided some of his countrymen in eluding their
enemy. On his flight he met Nicolas Le Challeux, an old carpenter
and lay preacher who had been amazed by his own ability to leap
over the fort's wall and save himself from death. He credited his
unusual strength to God. The strong religious beliefs of the Huguenots are illustrated by Le Challeux's account of his escape.

*I was myself surprised, going to my duty with my clasp knife
in my hand; for upon leaving my cabin I met the enemy, and saw
no other means of escape but turning my back, and making the
utmost possible haste to leap over the palisades, for I was closely
pursued, step by step, by a pikeman, and one with a partisan; and
I do not know how it was, unless by the grace of God, that my
strength was redoubled, old man as I am and grey headed, a thing
which at any other time I could not have done, for the rampart was
raised eight or nine feet; I then hastened to secret myself in the
woods. . . . From this place all the fort, even the inner court was
distinctly visible to me, looking there I saw a horrible butchery of
our men taking place and three standards of our enemies planted
upon the ramparts. Having then lost all hope of seeing our men
rally, I resigned all my senses to the Lord. . . . I discovered one of
our people, named Sieur de la Blonderie and a little behind him
another named Maître Robert, well known to us all, because he
had charge of the prayers at the fort. Immediately afterwards we
found also . . . many others. . . . One of our number . . . proposed
. . . would it not be better to fall into the hands of men than into
jaws of wild beasts or die of hunger in a strange land? I pointed
out . . . we should be cowards to trust in men rather than in God,*

*who gives life to his own in the midst of death, and gives ordinarily his assistance when the hopes of men entirely fail.*

*I also brought to their minds examples from Scripture, instancing Joseph, Daniel, Elias, and the other prophets, as well also the apostles, as St. Peter and St. Paul, who were all drawn out of much affliction, as would appear by means extraordinary and strange to the reason and judgment of men. His arm, said I is not shortened, nor in any wise enfeebled; His power is always the same. Do you not recollect said I, the flight of the Israelites before Pharaoh? What hope had that people of escaping from the hands of that powerful tyrant? He had them, as it were, under his heel. Before them they had the sea, on either side inaccessible mountains.*

*What then? He who opened the sea to make a path for his people, and made it afterwards to swallow up his enemies, cannot he conduct us by the forest places of this strange country? While thus discoursing, six of the company followed out the first proposition, and abandoned us to go and yield themselves up to our enemies, hoping to find favor before them. But they learned, immediately and by experience, what folly it is to trust more in men than in the promises of the Lord. . . . They were at once killed and massacred, and then drawn to the banks of the river, where the others killed at the fort lay in heaps. . . .*

*We perceived among the briars a body of men whom we at first thought to be enemies, who had gone there to cut us off; but, upon close observation, they seemed in as sad a plight as ourselves, naked and terrified; and we immediately perceived that they were our own people. It was Captain Laudonnière, his maid servant, Jacques Morgues of Dieppe [the artist], Francis Duval of Rouen, son of him of the iron crown of Rouen, Niguese de la Cratte, Nicholas the carpenter, the trumpeter of Sieur Laudonnière, and others who all together made the number of twenty six men. . . . In order to reach the banks of the stream it was necessary for us to traverse the briars and two other rivers similar to those which we passed the previous day; in order to accomplish which, the pole I had cut the day before was both useful and necessary, and the two others which Sr. de Laudonnière had provided; and we came pretty near to the vessel, but our hearts failed us from hunger and fatigue, and we should have remained where we were unless the sailors had given us a hand. . . .*

*We thereupon concluded that we could do no better than re-turn to France, and were of the opinion that the company should divide into two parts, the one remaining on board the Pearl, and the other under charge of Captain Maillard. . . . On Friday, the twenty fifth day of the month of September, we departed from this coast . . . and after the first day our two ships were so far separated we did not again encounter each other.*[26]

In all, between fifty and sixty Frenchmen escaped from the Spaniards. Jacques Ribault, son of Jean Ribault, sailed the *Pearl* back to France with Le Challeux aboard. Laudonnière went back on the *Greyhound* and landed in Wales. The young Ribault had been anchored in the river near Fort Caroline at the time of the onslaught. He had been deterred from entering the fray because of the danger of firing on his own countrymen. Perhaps the brutality of the Spaniards gave him little enthusiasm for fighting. The French recorded that the Spaniards took the eyes of the dead and flicked them from the points of their daggers in the direction of the French ships. Without boats, Menéndez could not attack the French vessels of Jacques Ribault and the latter was able to save those who escaped the Fort Caroline massacre.

Jean Ribault and most of his shipwrecked men never returned to their homeland. Thrown onto the beach near present-day Daytona Beach, the wet and unarmed survivors existed on seafood as they marched north in the attempt to reach Fort Caroline. At Matanzas the swift, deep inlet stopped their northward progress.

Meanwhile Indians brought news of the starving French strag-glers to Menéndez. He led 50 soldiers down Anastasia Island to Matanzas Inlet. In negotiations with the French, he promised them whatever mercy God would direct. Perhaps reassured by this prom-ise, the shipwrecked men surrendered, were ferried ten at a time over the water, and fed a good meal. Then Menéndez demanded that they submit to having their hands bound behind their backs. The reason for this act, he said, was the small number of his men in comparison to the 150 Frenchmen. The Spaniard sent the Catholics, artisans, and musicians under guard to St. Augustine. At Menéndez' signal, the others were run through with pike, sword, and dagger.

Captain Ribault was not with these unfortunates, but some

days later Menéndez learned that an even larger number of Frenchmen were on the south shore of Matanzas Inlet. Again he marched
to the scene. This time Ribault was among the stranded Frenchmen. Menéndez refused the offer of a large ransom for sparing
Ribault's life and sending him back to France. The Spanish commander repeated his promise that whatever mercy God would direct
would be shown to them. Ribault and approximately 200 of his
followers accepted. The rest of the Frenchmen, perhaps 150, decided
to take their chances with the vicissitudes of nature rather than
with God's will as interpreted by Menéndez and began walking with
painful strides south along the beach. Menéndez ferried Ribault and
his companions across the inlet and repeated his bloody perform-
ance of some days before.

Solís de Merás, a Spanish priest and eyewitness to the scene.
described the massacre in the following words:

*The Adelantado [Menéndez], taking Jean Ribault behind the
sand hills, among the bushes where the others had their hands tied
behind them, he said to these and all others as he had done before,
that they had four leagues to go after night, and that he could not
permit them to go unbound; and after they were all tied, he asked
if they were Catholics or Lutherans, or if any of them desired to
make confession.*

*Jean Ribault replied, "that all who were there were of the new
religion," and he then began to repeat the psalm, "Domine!
Memento Mei"; and having finished, he said, "that from dust they
came and to dust they must return, and that in twenty years, more
or less, he must render his final account; and that the Adelantado
might do with them as he chose." The Adelantado then ordered all
to be killed, in the same order and at the same mark, as had been
done to the others. He spared only the fifers, drummers and trumpeters, and four others who said that they were Catholics.[27]*

The man who actually killed Ribault first inquired of him
whether the French commander did not expect his soldiers to obey
orders. Ribault answered, "Yes." Then the Spaniard said, "I propose to obey the orders of my commander also. I am ordered to kill
you." The psalm that Ribault recited before the dagger was thrust
into his body was the 132nd Psalm which begins "Lord, remember

David"; but Ribault began it, according to an eyewitness, with "Lord, remember me."

According to some early accounts, Ribault's beard and a piece of his skin were sent to Philip II and the Frenchman's head was cut into four parts, which were penetrated by lances and raised at each corner of the Spanish fort at St. Augustine. In reporting to King Philip II, Menéndez stated: "I think it great good fortune that this man be dead, for the King of France could accomplish more with him and fifty thousand ducats than with other men and five hundred thousand ducats; and he could do more in one year, than another in ten. . . ." Menéndez thus disclosed that his real purpose was to push the French out of Florida and retain the territory in the undisputed possession of Spain.

Menéndez stressed his concerns for empire and pointed out that a French colony in Florida would seriously endanger Spanish commerce with the New World.[28] He also expressed the fear that the French would attempt to free the slaves in the Spanish colonies. He observed that his judgment in these matters was confirmed by the statements of a French captive from Fort Caroline, who admitted that the Frenchmen had planned to take and hold the strategic strait of Los Martyres, and Menéndez added that "from there they would take Havana, free all the negroes; that they would then send to make the same offer to the Spanish of Porto Rico and all other colonies." The Spanish Adelantado had previously informed his king that there were "in each of these islands more than thirty negroes to each Christian" and that "there are so many cunning and sagacious ones who desire this liberty." Undoubtedly Menéndez was cruel and bigoted, but he was a product of his era. He hated Lutherans, Huguenots, and other members of the new religious sects and showed them no mercy, but he was a patriotic Spaniard. To have saved the captives at Fort Caroline and the other Frenchmen who surrendered at Matanzas would have endangered the Spanish settlement at St. Augustine and Spanish control of the rest of Florida. Fed and restored to their manly vigor, the forces of Ribault might have broken their chains and taken over St. Augustine. Furthermore, Menéndez did not have supplies of food to sustain his soldiers and settlers as well as hundreds of French captives.

He treated the women and children taken at Fort Caroline well; and later when the Frenchmen who had refused to surrender to him at Matanzas did so at Cape Canaveral, he was their compassionate conqueror. The sixteenth century was not an age of respect for human life. But the twentieth century has no claim to morality in this respect. The bloody excesses of the Spanish civil war, Hitler's Germany, the Russians, and the Chinese demonstrate that man's inhumanity to man still exists in the modern age.

The settlement at Fort Caroline bequeathed many things to present-day Americans. The French colony was the first settlement of men and women within the confines of the United States that emphasized the right of man to worship God in freedom. At St. Johns Bluff one of the first churches in the New World was built by Menéndez. It was constructed from the planks which had been hewed for a Huguenot boat. The road which Menéndez cleared from St. Augustine to Fort Caroline became the first regularly and continuously used highway in what is now the United States. San Mateo, the Spanish name for Fort Caroline, continued as a fort and a mission, and from it were sent in 1566 the first colonists to Virginia. The combat at Fort Caroline was the first international conflict between white people within territory which became a part of the United States of America. Some of the captives taken at Fort Caroline, Matanzas, and Cape Canaveral remained in Florida to mingle with other colonists and sire children whose descendants are American citizens. The author has heard of two present-day Florida families which trace their descent from the French Huguenots of 1565, and complete records would doubtless reveal a larger number of contemporary Floridians with Huguenot ancestors.

# VI

# *"The Countess" Saves the Captain*

HE *Greyhound* on which Laudonnière escaped from the wrath of Menéndez at Fort Caroline sailed into St. George's Channel on November 10, 1565, and entered the nearby port of Swansea, Wales. He and the other survivors had crossed the ocean with meager supplies of food and water. They needed clothing and money to continue their homeward journey. After arranging for provisions for the ship and speeding it toward France, Laudonnière and some of his companions traveled overland from Wales into England. On the first night they reached Morgan, where the lord of the castle put them up for six or seven days while they recuperated from their arduous voyage. Like the men who returned on the *Pearl*, these Frenchmen suffered relapses in health on reaching land. Le Challeux reported that many people aboard the *Pearl* died soon after reaching France. Laudonnière recorded: "I was incontinently on land, where, after I had taken the ayre, a sickness took mee whereof I thought I should have dyed."

Rested and with some of his accustomed robust health restored, he proceeded to Bristol and to London. At the latter city Paul de Foix, the French ambassador to England, lent him money. Laudonnière crossed the channel to Calais and finally reached Paris. There he learned that the king was at his estate in Moulins, and Laudonnière did not see his monarch until the Ides of March, 1566. There are a number of possible explanations for Laudonnière's delay in reporting to the king. Perhaps he feared that Queen Mother Catherine might take his life as a gesture of good will toward Philip II of Spain, or have Laudonnière executed for his failure to hold Fort Caroline for France. In the ever-changing religious and political situations within France, he might fall as a Huguenot martyr

45

to Catholic power, and he did not know exactly what influence his friend Coligny had with Catherine in 1566. It seems reasonable to assume that both Laudonnière's uncertainty as to his treatment and his poor health prevented him from hurrying to the court of King Charles IX.

But Laudonnière did not pass his time in idleness. Probably at Morgan's castle in Wales he began his account of the voyage to Florida, the Fort Caroline settlement, and its destruction. In the Introduction to his *Notable History of Florida*, he declared it was folly to attempt settlement in America without adequate support from the mother country, "As within these few daies past the French have proved to my great griefe." His account of his stewardship was specifically planned to be presented to Charles IX. The time required for its completion may have been an additional reason for Laudonnière's delay in presenting himself to his king.

Meanwhile Catherine of France and Philip of Spain quarreled over their respective rights in Florida. On receiving Menéndez's report, Philip said: "He has done well." Rather than threatening Spain for her massacre of the Huguenots, Charles IX of France summoned Francisco de Alava, the Spanish ambassador, on November 23, 1565, and received him cordially. Alava demanded an audience with the Queen Mother and wrote Philip that the young Charles.

*took me by the hand and did not leave me until he conducted me to his mother's chamber. His mother was also surrounded by heretics and Catholics and many people. She received me with the same demonstrations with which her son had received me, but not wishing to give me a private audience, saw me there, in public, drawing her son very close to her and causing me to draw near also. I began to repeat the subjects of Your Majesty's letter, when I had so severe a chill that I had to take out the paper I carried with me and begin to read it. I was as little able to do that, and finally they called l'Aubespine, but not finding him, Saint Sulpice had to read it. The Queen held her head so that the company could not well see her face and assumed a very melancholy expression until the subject of the Imperial alliances was reached, when she lighted up a little and said that it seemed well to her. We then began upon the matter of Florida, upon which Saint Sulpice attempted to comment before she had answered. I observed that I had come to converse with them, and hoped they would be contented with Saint Sulpice's reading of the paper, and so they dismissed him. The Queen would nòt allow me to say a word on the subject, at one moment telling me, "The subjects of my son are going only to a mountainous region called Hercules discovered by the French crown over two hundred years ago." I turned to the King and began to enlarge upon the matter with the urgency which Your Majestry had directed me to use. The Queen's eyes kindled and she poised herself like a lioness to hear what I was saying to her son. I said in substance that it was a business of great consequence and that he should beseech his mother to weigh it well. At this she grew angry with me, and to tell Your Majesty the truth, I did the same with her, for she would not answer to the point and feigned wonder at everything I said. At last, closing her eyes, she exclaimed that for the life of her she understood nothing of this matter. By this Your Majestry can see with what sincerity she deals.*[29]

On January 15, 1566, after Jacques Ribault had reported to the French Court, Catherine met Alava again. This time she told the Spanish ambassador that she believed the French, who had gone to the "Isle des Bretons," had returned. Angered by this subterfuge, Alava replied, "I know of no Isles des Bretons. You can baptise the country 'Isles des Bretons' and call Peru 'Tierra firme des Bretons,' as you like, but I heard the order given to your captain to go to New France by way of Florida, in which the name Florida was used." Catherine tried to turn the conversation to other subjects, and showed her displeasure by a gesture of her head.

When Laudonnière finally presented himself at court on March 15, 1566, King Charles was cool toward him. An early account (Jacques de Thou, *Histoire Universelle*, London, 1734, in French from the Latin edition of 1606) stated that "il ne fut pas trop bien reçu," or that he was not well received. This simple statement was later distorted to the extent that historians declared carelessly and erroneously that Laudonnière was very badly received, or even that he retired in despair among his family, or that he did nothing of any consequence thereafter.

Nothing could be farther from the truth. Rather than retiring into obscurity after the capture of Fort Caroline, Laudonnière was

immediately in the center of irate Frenchmen who talked of revenge. At the French Court some men advocated an undeclared
naval war and the sinking of Spanish ships wherever found. The
petition of the widows and orphans of the massacred men at Fort
Caroline, asking Charles to demand redress from Philip II further
aroused patriotic Frenchmen.[30] Laudonnière gave the Queen Mother
reasons why France should hold New France, and his Spanish interpreter (who had been kept under guard at Fort Caroline) was
interviewed by Catherine in the presence of the Cardinal of Bourbon to confirm the reports of gold and pearls in Florida. The interpreter secretly reported this interview to Spanish Ambassador
Alava.

Laudonnière, Jacques Ribault, Sandoval, and others planned
an expedition to attack the Spanish colonies. Sandoval was the
piratical governor of Belle-Isle-en-Mer off the Brittany coast who
had gained considerable wealth in ships and money by plundering
Spanish commerce. Alava complained to Catherine, but she put off
his protests. Laudonnière was so poor, she said, that she gave him
fifty crowns. Obviously he did not have the means to finance a voyage. On his return from France, Ribault had not known of the massacre of his father's forces and certainly could not be arming ships;
and as for the interpreter, he was only a poor beggar, a charity
patient at the Moulins hospital whom Catherine claimed she had
never seen.

Whether the Queen Mother did or did not prevent Laudonnière from avenging the Fort Caroline massacre is not known. From
her point of view and for the good of diplomatic relations with
Spain, it was better for some man other than Laudonnière to head
an expedition against Spanish Florida. Although Catherine avowed
that she was not involved in fitting out ships for Dominique de
Gourgues in 1567, the Catholic De Gourgues rather than the Protestant Laudonnière avenged the honor of France. In 1568 he arrived in Florida to lead his 180 men against the Spaniards at San
Mateo. Guided by a Frenchman who had been living with the Indians of the area, the French force cut their feet marching through
the oyster-shell marshes to surprise the Spaniards while they sat
picking their teeth after a meal. Hundreds of them were slain and

others captured. The latter were hanged and written on a sign placed above their bodies was, "Not as to Spaniards, but as to Traitors, Robbers, and Murderers."

The Indians welcomed the Frenchmen and sang songs which they had learned from the Huguenots at Caroline, including "Happy Is One To Be A Volunteer For God." One old Indian woman claimed she could die in peace now that the French had returned, but her happiness was of short duration. De Gourgues's motive was revenge, not settlement. After restoring the Fort Caroline name, he sailed away and the Spaniards reoccupied their San Mateo fort.

The dramatic and cruel revenge of Fort Caroline made a national hero of De Gourgues. On the other hand the mounting opposition to Protestantism in France was making life increasingly precarious for Laudonnière. In 1569 the Prince of Condé, the leading figure of the Huguenots, was treacherously slain after surrendering in battle. King Henry of Navarre became the titular head of the Huguenot party, but for a few years Admiral Coligny still exercised the real leadership. In 1570 the Treaty of St. Germain once more confirmed the grant of limited toleration to Protestants. Throughout these troublesome times, Laudonnière clung steadfastly and courageously to his religious faith. For a time he was employed by the Cardinal of Bourbon, Archbishop of Rouen, in sailing in American waters on the 120-ton *Countess Testu*. The royal arsenals at Havre-de-Grâce were the sources of his artillery. On September 28, 1570, Charles IX ordered the treasurer and keeper of the royal artillery at Havre-de-Grâce to extend a loan of four bronze cannon to Laudonnière and give him thirty rounds of ammunition for each of the guns. According to the king's order, Laudonnière had used the guns on a recent voyage to the West Indies and the loan of them was to enable him to make another trip to the New World. Since he was a man of the sea, he undoubtedly enjoyed the command of a ship and evidently used it in attacking Spanish commercial vessels.

At least Alava made a violent attack on him in August, 1571, to the Cardinal of Bourbon. Louis d'Este, the ambassador of the Pope, was there when Alava gave vent to his rage against "one Laudonnière sponsored by the Cardinal." The latter declared that he would not support Laudonnière if he had done wrong, "but since he had not done anything wrong he would support and favor him." Infuriated, Alava reminded the prelate that a papal order had named the cardinal as one of the three inquisitors of France "to do away with all the heretics." Catherine de Medici observed that the Spaniard's insult "greatly offended Monsieur le Cardinal because he hates the heretics," and she added that Alava "was born to bring grief to everyone."[31]

In 1572 Laudonnière was the principal in a nautical enterprise to America. By a contract recently found at La Rochelle, he signed on May 16, 1572, to command an expedition to America (described as a trip to the Indies of Peru) to navigate along the coasts and among the ports of the New World and "to conduct traffic in merchandise business, to sell, exchange and barter the merchandise" aboard the vessel. The contract obligated all concerned in the venture to defer to Captain Laudonnière under penalty of "being treated as felons and rebels against the King." According to the document, "all the above persons promise that they will not make any boarding, piracy, misdeed or grief to the friends, allies or subjects of the King, our sovereign lord, and giving them aid and comfort if needed and required."

Laudonnière, who resided in Paris in 1572, was to be master of the *Countess Testu* and furnish a third of her cargo. He was the only man to receive one-third of the profits. The other two-thirds was to be divided among a list of people of importance in France who were parties to the contract. The commander was charged with bringing back exotic birds and animals from America and half of the profits from their importation were to go to Laudonnière. But he was to share his part with those who supplied food and the remaining one-half was to go to the third parties. The voyage was definitely a commercial venture rather than a piratical one, and it had some overtones of a scientific nature.

The *Countess Testu* was on the roadstead of Chef de Bois (three miles out from La Rochelle and now called Pointe de Chef de Baye) and ready to put to sea on May 26, 1572. Soon thereafter the ship sailed on her mission. The results of the voyage are not known, but this enterprise undoubtedly saved Laudonnière's life.

After the Peace of St. Germain, Coligny acquired great influence with the king who began to demonstrate some independence of his mother, Catherine. Resolved to make his country stronger, Charles planned to keep the terms of the recent treaty to satisfy the Huguenots and weld all Frenchmen together by a firm policy toward Spain. His first step toward unity was arranging a marriage between his sister Margaret and Henry of Navarre. On August 18, 1572, Huguenots swarmed into Paris to attend the wedding of Henry. This celebration was more than the extreme Catholics under the Guises could stand. They and the Queen Mother, angered because Coligny had taken her place with her son, hired an assassin who fired at Coligny on August 22 and severely wounded the Huguenot leader. Charles rushed to Coligny's bedside. "Yours the wound, mine the sorrow," he told his minister and promised to bring the assassin and his accomplices to justice.

Catherine and the Guises knew an investigation would show them to be the patrons of an assassin. To cover their complicity, they planned to get rid of Coligny and thousands of Huguenots, but they did not dare kill without the approval of the king. Catherine succeeded in winning back the favor of her son; he was not too bright and as changeable as a weather vane. The responsibility for the resulting massacre rested on Catherine and the Guises, and their agents were the passionate Catholics of Paris. Chalk marks were placed on the houses of Huguenots or the dwellings where they had rooms on the night of August 23.

Before dawn the next morning, the feast day of St. Bartholomew, the ringing of church bells was the signal for selected Catholics to begin the massacre of Huguenots. The wounded Coligny was one of the first victims of the bloody orgy, with the Duke of Guise directing the killing. Blood was shed all over Paris and bigoted Catholics in the provinces of France continued their killing of Huguenots for a number of days. The intense religious feeling of the times was illustrated by the fact that Pope Gregory XIII decreed a solemn Te Deum to be sung, and cold-blooded Philip II of Spain burst into his only recorded laughter on receiving news of the St. Bartholomew's Day Massacre.

As an intimate friend and follower of Coligny, Laudonnière

would certainly have died at the Admiral's side had he not been at sea on the *Countess Testu* on August 24, 1572. The date of Laudonnière's return to France is unknown. In fact until two years ago there was no evidence that he ever sailed back to his native land. But the discovery of a document which bears the only known signature of Laudonnière shows that he was alive and still in the service of his king in November of 1573. This document is a receipt for royal monies paid by Guillaume le Beau, treasurer of France, to Laudonnière for services as "The Captain of the Western Fleet." No later information about his activities has been found. It has been assumed that he lived until 1582 and perhaps he continued his captaincy of the western fleet until his death. In 1586 his *L'Histoire notable de la Floride* was published in Paris and the following year Richard Hakluyt translated it into English under the title of *A Notable Historie Containing Foure Voyages Made by Certayne French Captaynes into Florida.*

# VII

# *Remember Me, Remember David*

FFIGIES *Regum Ac Principum* by Crispin van de Passe was published in 1598. The last chapter contains an account of Laudonnière's work and a portrait of him. The encircling inscription reads, "The most noble René Laudonnière, commander of the French fleet in America." Under the reproduced picture is the inscription:

*Shall I, Laudonnière, pass away untouched by glory?*
*Florida, of the regions which now comprise America,*
*Is not the least of those subject to the glory of France.*
*If a treacherous band of friends had not disgracefully betrayed*
*This person to the enemy (a person who nevertheless has escaped*
*from all injuries, from all hands) what things,*
*What manner of things, and how many things I might*
*have accomplished!*

Directly under the portrait is also the sentence, "There is nothing entirely lucky." Certainly Laudonnière was lucky in escaping from Fort Caroline and in being at sea at the time of the Massacre of St. Bartholomew's Day. But it was training and industry rather than luck that gives him stature in history.

Did his deeds justify a place in glory for him? He was the founder and governor of France's Fort Caroline in Florida, but the Huguenot settlement was wiped out by Menéndez. Yet the attempt at French colonization led to the establishment of St. Augustine, the first permanent European settlement within present-day America. St. Augustine, in turn, stimulated Great Britain to send colonists to Roanoke Island and later to establish a colony at Jamestown. Furthermore, the Fort Caroline settlement set a new pattern for religious freedom in America—a pattern which was to be imitated until religious liberty and personal freedom became the great trademark of the United States. The beginnings of the Declaration of Inde-

53

pendence and the Constitution of the United States stemmed from the spirit of freedom exemplified by Laudonnière at Fort Caroline, and these documents still contain the greatest revolutionary statements of human rights by a government of free men known to the world.

What conclusions must the fair observer reach about Laudonnière's command at Fort Caroline? Certainly he was a loyal servant of his king. As he conceived his duty, his task was not to establish a self-sufficient agricultural community. The crown had promised to supply Fort Caroline, and Laudonnière worked diligently to find the raw materials needed by France, especially the precious metals. His struggle to discover these resources and the failure of the mother country to send foodstuffs were major causes of difficulties with the Indians and the impatient colonists. His dedication to the idea of a permanent colony is illustrated by two actions: his refusal to allow his hungry settlers to devour the chickens which were needed to stock the land for the future, and his rejection of Sir John Hawkins' offer to transport the disillusioned settlers back to France. Furthermore, he allowed no countryman to reveal to Hawkins that gold and pearls had been found in Florida. To have done so would have stimulated the interest of the Englishman and endangered the French control of Florida. Laudonnière also opposed the members of his colony who wished to engage in piratical expeditions against Spanish commerce. These forays, he knew, would bring retaliation from Spain with a consequent danger to Caroline.

As an administrator he did at one time lose control of the colony. In any fair evaluation, however, the composition of the settlers should be considered. Some of them were political hotheads and others were former prisoners. Most of these demanded quick sources of wealth. Not finding an abundance of gold and silver, they turned to plundering the treasure-laden ships of Spain. The character of the mutineers was illustrated by their planning an attack on a Spanish town in the Caribbean at the time that the settlers would be at religious services celebrating Christmas.

In religion he maintained one of the colony's purposes in providing a haven for people seeking religious liberty. While the basic principles of individual faith and religious freedom were maintained, he also insisted on having daily religious services. He began his settlement with prayer and songs of worship. Laudonnière's account states:

*On the morrow about the breake of day, I commanded a trumpet to be sounded, that being assembled we might give God thankes for our favourable and happie arrivall. There wee sang a Psalme of thanksegiving unto God, beseeching him that it would please him of his grace to continue his accustomed goodnesse toward us his poore servants, and ayde us in all our enterprises, that all might turne to his glory and the advancement of our King. The prayer ended, every man began to take courage.*

Laudonnière had the courage to follow his convictions, for despite endangering his life, he clung to his Protestant faith. For him God did not intervene in all matters of man. Thus Fort Caroline fell not because of God's displeasure, but because France failed to supply it and Ribault did not utilize his fighting forces to the best advantage of the colonists. Laudonnière firmly believed that God would punish men for their sins and bless them for their good deeds. After the mutineers had returned to Caroline where they were tried and found guilty, he told them before their execution:

*While you thought to escape the justice of men, you could not avoid the judgment of God, which is a thing by no meanes to be avoided hath led you, and in spight of you hath made you arrive in this place, to make you confesse how true his judgments are, and that he never suffereth so foule a fault to escape unpunished.*

In recalling the plight of the men left by Ribault at Charlesfort in 1562, Laudonnière wrote:

*Whereupon our men being farre from all succors, found themselves in such extremitie that without the ayd of Almighty God, the onely searcher of the hearts and thoughts of men, which never forsaketh those that seeke him in their afflictions, they had bene quite cleane out of all hope. . . .*

*But misfortune or rather the just judgment of God would have it, that those which could not be overcome by fire nor water, should be undone by their owne selves.*

Undoubtedly his faith bolstered his courage and made helpfulness a part of his character. His personal courage was demonstrated by his actions at Fort Caroline. When facing overwhelming odds and racked by illness, he fought the Spaniards with all of his physical power. Being pointed out by the traitor, Francis Jean, Laudonnière bore the brunt of the concentrated attack by Spanish soldiers but did not retreat until all hope of success was gone. Even in flight he had the presence of mind to gather wooden staves to support other escapees who could not swim to safety. Good swimmer that he was, he needed no extra support, but he did not fail to think of the needs of his companions. His first concern after returning to Europe was for the welfare of those who escaped the Fort Caroline massacre. In military defeat, he turned to God. "The next morning [after the flight from Caroline], I betooke me to my prayers with the souldier which was with me." Laudonnière also recorded, "I made my prayer unto God, and thanked him of his grace which he had shewed unto my poore souldiers which were escaped."

Religious conviction evidently tempered Laudonnière's opinions regarding the leadership of Ribault. The relationship between the two men was cordial at Fort Caroline. But when the latter offered Laudonnière retention of command while Ribault established another settlement, Laudonnière preferred returning to France to report on his stewardship in the New World to accepting a demotion. It is reasonable to assume that Laudonnière noted the differences between Ribault and himself. What would have been the outcome of the struggle between France and Spain for Florida had Ribault heeded Laudonnière's warning of the danger from hurricanes and made a stand at defensible Fort Caroline? Yet Ribault certainly treated the man he supplanted in command at Fort Caroline with kindness and respect during the days they had together. Knowing the accusations and gossip against him at the French court, Laudonnière must have appreciated this treatment by his fellow Huguenot. In his history of Florida, Laudonnière blamed the French government for failing to send provisions and men, not the strategy of Ribault, for the loss of Fort Caroline.

History has justifiably recognized the greatness of Jean Ribault. He and his followers chose to die for principle rather than recant and abandon their religion. No such choice was presented to Laudonnière. His alternatives were to fight until his cause was lost and then escape, or to stand alone against 500 Spanish soldiers and die a martyr's death. After escaping but still facing death from starvation or wild animals, he chose to rely on his resources and his faith rather than to surrender to Menéndez. Laudonnière lived to serve his country for many years and continued steadfast to his principles despite the personal danger involved in remaining a Huguenot.

Historians have treated Laudonnière in different ways. In *Les Trois Mondes* which was published at Paris in 1582, Henri Lancelot Voisin describes the slaughter at Fort Caroline and criticizes the French commander. "They [the Spaniards] killed them with their spears while they were sleeping in their beds at dawn; except Laudonnière who, followed by his page boy, leaped over the palisade and saved himself. He left behind him to carry the burden of his faults his soldiers and others who were as lax at their guard as was their chief." However, the author of *Effigies Regum Ac Principum* considered Laudonnière to be one of the great men of the sixteenth century and placed a portrait of him in the book. On the other hand, he only mentioned Ribault in passing and gave him neither picture nor biographical sketch. Laudonnière was a dignified and noble man to Léon Guérin, author of *Les Navigateurs français*. To Guérin, Laudonnière showed heroic courage in his defense of Fort Caroline and "magnanimous beyond expression" was his assistance to his companions in their flight from the overwhelming odds which confronted them. Guérin declared that even the Spaniards had to admit Laudonnière's "devotion, cool headedness and heroism." It is also noteworthy that the great sixteenth and seventeenth century English geographer, Richard Hakluyt, considered Laudonnière's history of Florida a significant contribution to geographic knowledge and translated it into the English language. Hakluyt was active in promoting British exploration and colonization of North America and believed the account of France in Florida by Laudonnière would be beneficial to English sea captains and colonial leaders.

"Shall I pass away untouched by glory?" asked Laudonnière. Human beings yearn for a touch of glory, and most of them receive at least a bit of it in the sympathetic understanding of a wife or husband, or from the confidence of their children. Few men, how-

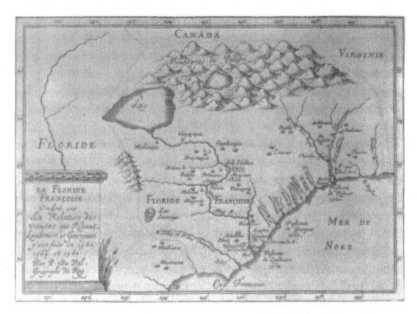

Laudonnière's "French Florida" as depicted by Pierre DuVal in a 1665 map. It is notable that the boundaries carefully embraced for France the Appalachian Mountains, accurately identified by Laudonnière as the best source of gold and other minerals in the general area of Fort Caroline.

ever, go down the ages with an aura of greatness. Laudonnière was not one of these fortunate few, but his faith and his courage can offer inspiration to individuals who study his life. Though Fort Caroline fell, his effort to establish a permanent French colony in Florida, a colony to provide its settlers with freedom of religion and economic opportunity, gives him more than a touch of glory.

In Duval County and its major city of Jacksonville, Florida, the name of Jean Ribault is perpetuated in school, street, geographic area, club, and in many other ways. But Laudonnière has not been given the recognition which his place in history deserves. In the region where he built Fort Caroline, Spaniard, Englishman, and American strove to build civilizations which might endure. In the Civil War, Northerner and Southerner battled to control the land. Today the large city of Jacksonville, the gateway to Florida, stands not many miles from the former location of Caroline. Near the spot of that French fortification the Fort Caroline National Memorial is, in part, a memorial to René de Laudonnière.

In the 132nd Psalm King David pledged himself to find an habitation for God. In a sense Laudonnière was a sixteenth century David seeking a place in the New World where God might be worshiped in freedom. Just before he was killed, Ribault chanted the 132nd Psalm but changed "Lord, remember David, to "Lord, remember me." Perhaps God remembered by allowing Ribault to occupy a glorious place in history; but Laudonnière would have been justified in musing: "Yes, Ribault could assuredly ask that God remember him alone; but as for me Laudonnière, who like David, had many faults, I pray: 'Lord, remember me; Lord, remember David.' "

# NOTES

1. Crispin van de Passe, *Effigies Regum* (Colonia Agrippina, 1598).
2. Nicolas Le Challeux, *Last Voyage of Ribaut* (London, Drummond, 1566); also in George R. Fairbanks, *The History and Antiquities of the City of St. Augustine* (New York, C. B. Norton, 1858), p. 42.
3. Léon Guérin, *Les Navigateurs français* (Paris, Bertrand, 1847), p. 180.
4. The exact boundaries of an extensive area called Loudonois are shown in a 1707 map of Poitou by A. H. Iallot (Map Division of Library of Congress). The area and its central town of Loudon are shown in various 16th century maps. For a geographic and historic description of the substantially Protestant Loudon, see C. M. Saugrain, *Dictionnaire Universel de la France* (Paris, 1726). This town can be found on today's maps at longitude O degrees, latitude 47 degrees north.
5. Part Two, X, p. 132.
6. E. T. Hamy, "Le Capitaine René de Laudonnière—Nouveaux renseignements sur ses navigations, 1561-1572," *Bulletin de géographie historique et descriptive* (Paris, Leroux, 1902), p. 53.
7. Brooks MSS, dated Sept. 23, 1561, Library of Congress MSS. Ac. 134.
8. Charles W. Baird, *History of the Huguenot Emigration to America* (New York, Dodd, Mead & Co., 1885), pp. 25, 60; Francis Parkman, *Pioneers of France in the New World* (Boston, Little, Brown & Co., 1865), I, 21.
9. Part Two, VII, p. 99.
10. Jean Ribaut, *The Whole and True Discouerye of Terra Florida* (London, Hall, 1563).
11. Part Two, IV, pp. 81-82.   12. Part Two, II, p. 72.   13. Part Two, X, p. 132.
14. Le Challeux, *Last Voyage of Ribaut*, p. 40; also in George R. Fairbanks, *The History and Antiquities of the City of St. Augustine* (New York, C. B. Norton, 1858). At page 45 of Fairbanks an encounter with a bison is mentioned. For other references to bison in Florida in the early colonial period, see H. B. Sherman, "The Occurrence of Bison in Florida," *Quarterly Journal of the Florida Academy of Sciences*, XVII, 228-32.

60    LAUDONNIERE & FORT CAROLINE

15. René Laudonnière, *L'Histoire notable de la Floride* (Paris, Basanier, 1586) ; see also Daniel G. Brinton, "The Precious Metals Possessed by the Early Florida Indians," in *Notes on the Floridian Peninsula* (Philadelphia, Sabin, 1859) ; see also *Georgia Mineral Newsletter*, Vol. XIII, No. 4, concerning a 16th century funeral urn top recently found near these mines.

The principal source of domestic gold in the United States for minting coins and other purposes, prior to the California gold rush of 1849, was in the Georgia and North Carolina section of the Appalachian Mountains (A. M. Bateman, *Economic Mineral Deposits* [New York, Wiley, 1942]).

Two accounts by Floridians about the gold mines which were discovered in the Fort Caroline area and not mentioned in the text of this book are found in the 1904 edition of the Hakluyt Society Publications, *Voyages*, as follows. At page 113 of Vol. IX the deposition of Nicholas Borgoignon (the French piper from Fort Caroline captured by Sir Francis Drake at St. Augustine) quotes the Frenchman as saying that the mineral-bearing mountains "shine so bright in the day in some places that they cannot behold them, and therefore they travel unto them by night." He also describes a large diamond found in that locality and speaks of other diamonds, rubies, etc. Until recent years gems were in fact extracted in this area on a commercial basis, and your author has found rubies, sapphires, and garnets in these mountains in southwestern North Carolina. At page 112 of the same volume the deposition of Pedro Morales is found. He describes the mines and states that they were those revealed to Laudonnière by the Indians (see also page 383).

16. *Narrative of Le Moyne* (Boston, Osgood, 1875), translated by F. B. Perkins from the 16th century Latin work: Jacobo Le Moyne de Morgues, *Brevis Narratio* (Frankfort, de Bry, 1591). Reference is to page 4 of the 1875 publication.

17. Richard Hakluyt (ed.), *Voyages* (Glasgow, 1904), IX, 83. All other references to Laudonnière's statements come from this text.

18. Part Two, II, pp. 72-73.    19. *Narrative of Le Moyne*, p. 4.

20. John Sparke, Jr., *The Voyage Made by M. John Hawkins, Esq.*, in Richard Hakluyt (ed.), *Voyages* (London, 1810), III, 615.

21. Part Two, XI.    22. Part Two, V.

23. Gonzalo Solís de Merás, *Pedro Menéndez de Avilés*, trans. Jeannette Thurber Connor (DeLand, Fla., Florida State Historical Society, 1923), p. 104.

24. *Proceedings of the Massachusetts Historical Society* (Boston, Mass. Hist. Soc., 1892-4), 2nd series, VIII, 426.    25. *Ibid.*, p. 463.

26. Fairbanks, *History and Antiquities of St. Augustine*, p. 38.

27. *Ibid.*, p. 83.    28. Part Two, X.

29. Woodbury Lowery, *The Spanish Settlements Within the Present Limits of the United States; Florida, 1562-1574* (New York, Russell, 1959), p. 115.

30. Part Two, XIII. And, as an example of the period's propaganda for France's re-entry into the battle for Florida, see: *Haranque d'un Caicuque* (France, 1596). A photostatic copy is in the Fort Caroline National Memorial Library, Jacksonville, Florida.

31. *Lettres de Catherine de Médicis* (Paris, Imprimerie Nationale, 1880), X, 283. For a discussion of Laudonnière's various business allies in this period see Charles de La Roncière, *Histoire de la Marine Française* (Paris, Librairie Plon, 1910), IV, 123; and see the photographic copy of proceedings in a lawsuit concerning Laudonnière and a business associate (La Ploncet) now in the Fort Caroline National Memorial Library. Incidentally, this lawsuit records Laudonnière's last known residence to be in the resort of Saint-Germain-en-Laye, a suburb of Paris where the royal family also maintained a residence.

# THE DOCUMENTS

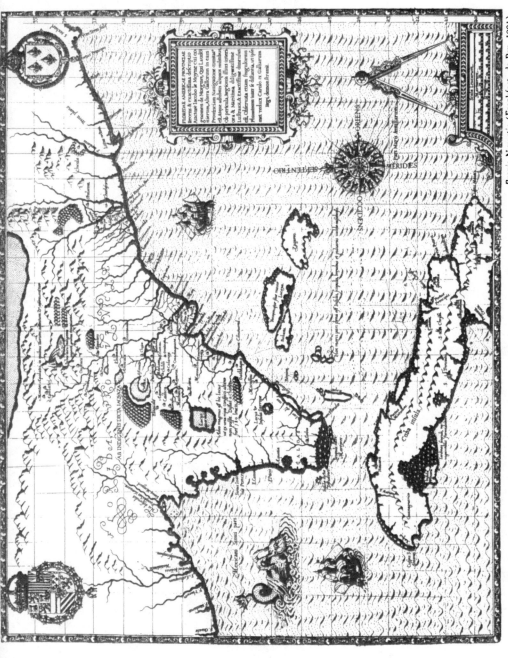

*Brevis Narratio* (Frankfort, de Bry, 1991)

Le Moyne's map of Florida.

# What They Said

EVERE limits are placed on history and biography by the sources available to a writer. One who delves into some aspect of contemporary history is confronted by a plethora of source material, but the investigator of the French attempt to establish a permanent colony in Florida in the sixteenth century longs for more documents, letters, and diaries. However, many Frenchmen of that century were literate individuals and some of them had a flair for writing. In addition, among the personnel of Spanish expeditions were official historians and literate priests. The Spaniards also took depositions from foreigners captured on Spanish-claimed lands. Sea captains, colonial administrators, and even a few settlers were so intrigued by the voyage to America and the wonders of the New World that they were moved to describe their unusual experiences to fellow Europeans. Frequently a colonial leader wrote a long report, or a history, to explain, defend, and justify his administrative ability. The total number of extant accounts of the French in Florida, therefore, is surprisingly large.

The purpose of this part of the book is to give the reader a taste of what Frenchmen and Spaniards wrote and thought about the events which took place in Florida in the 1560's. The reader should not be surprised by the variations in the accounts of eyewitnesses or by the exaggerations of some witnesses. At times he will also note differences between their statements and the historical-biography in Part One of this volume. By consulting and evaluating many sources the historian attempts to arrive at facts and present valid interpretations.

The longest account of the Fort Caroline settlement was written by René de Laudonnière in 1565 and 1566. His *L'Histoire*

63

*notable de la Floride* was published at Paris in 1586 and translated into English by Richard Hakluyt. The well-known British geographer's translation is rather difficult for modern readers because of the spelling used in the sixteenth and seventeenth centuries. The Hakluyt translation is in *The Principal Navigations, Voyages, Traffiques & Discoveries of the English Nation* (Glasgow, 1903-5), VIII, 439-86, and IX, 1-100. The carpenter at Fort Caroline, Nicolas Le Challeux, has an interesting personal account in his *Last Voyage of Ribaut* (London, 1566). Jean Ribault's story has been told, and updated, in a volume prepared by Mrs. Jeannette Thurber Connor: Jean Ribaut, *The Whole & True Discouerye of Terra Florida*, a facsimile reprint of the London edition of 1563, together with a transcript of an English version in the British Museum with notes by H. P. Biggar, and a biography by Jeannette Thurber Connor (DeLand, Florida State Historical Society, 1927). A moving narrative of Menéndez by a member of his force is in Jeannette Thurber Connor (ed. and trans.), *Pedro Menéndez de Avilés, Adelantado, Governor and Captain-General of Florida*, Memorial by Gonzalo Solís de Merás (DeLand, Florida State Historical Society, 1923). These two Connor volumes are now being reproduced by the University of Florida Press as part of its twelve-volume Quadricentennial Edition of the Floridiana Facsimile and Reprint Series. An excellent general secondary account of the Spanish and French in Florida is given in Woodbury Lowery, *The Spanish Settlements within the Present Limits of the United States, Florida 1562-1574* (New York, 1905). There are relatively few primary sources but many secondary sources available to students of this period.

The writings of Laudonnière, Ribault, Challeux, and Solís de Merás are well known and available. The documents and other sources herein presented have been taken from rare books printed in Latin, French, and Spanish. Most of these writings and others included here from manuscript sources have never before been translated into and printed in English. Unless otherwise specified, all the translations were made by the author of this book.

# I

# *Maytime*

A VERY HUMAN LETTER was written by a young Frenchman at Fort Caroline in 1564. At that time the French settlers were optimistic about the future of their colony. The writer tells of the voyage to Florida, describes the new country, and the beginnings of the settlement. The letter was originally published as a pamphlet in Paris in 1565, but is most readily available today in Henri Ternaux-Compans (ed.), *Voyages, relations et mémoires originaux pour servir à l'histoire de l'Amérique . . .* (Paris, 1841), pp. 233-45; entitled, "Coppie d'une lettre venant de la Floride, enuoyee a Rouen, et depuis au Seigneur D'Eueron; ensemble le plan et portraict du fort que les Francois y ont faict."

COPY OF A LETTER COMING FROM FLORIDA, SENT TO ROUEN
AND THEN TO M. D'EVERON, TOGETHER WITH THE PLAN AND
PICTURE OF THE FORT WHICH THE FRENCH BUILT THERE

*My very honored father: I arrived in this land of New France, prosperous and in good health (thank God), which I pray may also be true of you. I must not fail to take pen in hand and run it over the paper in order to give you a small description of the Isle of Florida, called New France, and of the type and customs of the Natives which you will please accept in good grace. But I ask you humbly to excuse me if I do not write more fully, as I would wish, for the reason is that we work every day on our fort which is now defending us.*

*We left Havre on April 22, under the command of Mr. René de Laudonnière, the gentleman from Poictevin, who is in charge of three warships. The one navigated by him is called "Isabel of Honfleur," whose captain was Jean Lucas, acting as admiral. The other ship, that the vice-admiral, Captain Vasseur of Dieppe, navigated, was called the "Little Breton," on which I embarked and made my voyage. The third ship was named the "Falcon" and was navigated by Captain Pierre Marchant. All these (with the aid of our good God who was with us) navigated together every day for a long time, not being more than three leagues apart, so that we can say (giving thanks to the Lord) that we had one of the most fortunate sea voy-*

*ages, owing to the great blessings bestowed by the Lord on us poor sinners; and we traveled successfully without running into any obstacle, except that, while sailing along the coast of England, we encountered about eighteen or twenty vessels which we thought to be English, which were waiting for a chance to capture us but soon discovered that we were ready, in battle position, to take them on, because we had been told prior to our departure that there would be some English ships lying in wait for us in order to capture us. When those vessels discovered us and saw all our ensigns deployed and our maintop in combat-readiness, we saw the admiral and the vice-admiral of those vessels, lining up the other vessels in formation; and then they came directly at us and we at them, and then we noticed that they were Flanders ships. We talked to them and they said that they were going to Brussels to load salt, and why wouldn't we let them go.*

*We continued on our course until June 22, when we came into view of New France, formerly called Florida, where we smelled the odoriferous aroma of many good things because of the wind which was coming from the land. Seeing the very flat land, without a single mountain, and in a very straight line along the sea and full of beautiful trees and woods along the seashore, I leave it to you to imagine the happiness we felt.*

*To the south we saw a beautiful river which prompted Mr. de Laudonnière to disembark and reconnoiter. We went, in fact, accompanied by only a dozen soldiers, and as soon as they set foot on land, three chiefs, together with more than four hundred Natives, came to greet Mr. de Laudonnière in their own way by flattering him as though paying tribute to an idol. Thereafter, the chiefs led him a short distance away (about an arrow's shot away) to where there was a beautiful bower of laurel, and there they sat down together and made signs expressing to Mr. de Laudonnière how happy they were that we had come, and also making signs (to Mr. de Laudonnière and the Sun) saying that he was the brother of the Sun and that he should go to war with them against their enemies whom they called TYMANGOUA. By making signs to us, by nodding their heads three times, they said that it was only a three-days journey. Mr. de Laudonnière promised them to go with them, and they each bowed and thanked each other, according to their status.*

*Shortly thereafter Mr. de Laudonnière wanted to go up the river once more and, looking upon a low sand dune, recognized a boundary marker of white stone into which the King's coat-of-arms was engraved, and which had been put up by Captain Jean Ribault, of Dieppe, on the first voyage which he had made. Mr. de Laudonnière was pleased and knew he was on the River May, the name which was given to it by Jean Ribault on his arrival, which was the first of May. And we stayed with the marker for half an hour and the Natives brought juice of the laurel and their excellent potions and, embracing the marker, all were chanting TYMANGOUA, as though wanting to say by so doing that they were going to be victorious over their enemies, whom they called TYMANGOUA, and that the Sun god had sent Mr. de Laudonnière, his brother, to avenge them. After giving them some presents Mr. de Laudonnière ordered the return aboard ship, leaving those poor people wailing and weeping about our departure. One of them even forced his way aboard and had gone to sleep there but was returned to land on Friday.*

*Then, after weighing anchor and skirting the coast until Sunday, we discovered a lovely river to which Mr. de Laudonnière sent Captain Vasseur, accompanied by ten soldiers of whom I was one. As soon as we were on land we found another chief with three of his sons and over two hundred Natives, their women and their little children. The chief was very ancient, and made signs to us saying that he had seen five generations, i.e., the children of his children, up to the fifth generation. After he had made us sit down under the laurel tree which was next to him, he made the sign for TYMAN-GOUA to us, just as the others. But as to the rest, they are the biggest thieves in the world because they can steal with their feet as well as with their hands, notwithstanding the fact that they are naked except for an animal skin covering their private parts. They are painted in black all over, in beautiful designs, and the women have some long strands of white moss wrapped around them covering their breasts and their private parts. They are very obedient to their husbands, not as thieving as they are, but they covet rings and chokers around their necks.*

*One day, after the river had been sounded, it was found deep enough for letting the ships enter, but not as deep as the River May so that Mr. de Laudonnière returned aboard ship and counseled with Captain Vasseur about returning to the River May. The following Tuesday we weighed anchor in order to go back there and arrived the following Friday, and immediately went ashore and were respectfully received by the Natives, like the first time, and were led to the same place where we are now building our fort, which is called Fort Caroline, and which was given that name because the King's name is Charles. You can see a picture of it below.*

*The fort is in the said River May, about six leagues up the river from the sea, which we will shortly have so well fortified as to have it defense-worthy, with very good conveniences and the water coming into the moat of the fort.*

*We even found a certain cinchona tree, which has dietary value, which is its least virtue; for the juice proceeding from it has such virtue that, when a thin man or woman drinks it regularly for some time, he or she would become very fat and stout; and it has also other good medicinal properties. We have learned from the doctors that it sells very well in France and that it is well liked.*

*Mr. de Laudonnière forbade our soldiers to send it aboard these ships, and only he would and did send some as a gift to the King and to the other Princes of France and to the Admiral, together with the gold which we had found there; but he gave permission to put in a supply for the first ships which would go back home so that, with the aid of the Lord, there will be a good supply of it, being sure that it will be much appreciated here and there. Mr. de Laudonnière wants, if there is a profit, that his soldiers should share in it.*

*We also found a certain kind of cinnamon, but not the best kind—somewhat too red—and also some rhubarb, though very little. However, we have hopes that in time we will be able to have the conveniences which might be had there.*

*Twenty-five leagues from our fort is a river which is called the Jordan and in which there are excellent martens, where we hope to go, with the aid of the Lord, within about six weeks. Furthermore, there are some very beautiful blood-red cedar trees, and the woods are filled with them, almost to the exclusion of anything else; and also there is an abundance of pine trees, and another kind of timber which is yellow; and even the woods are so full of vines that you can hardly take two steps forward without finding an abundance of grapes which are beginning to turn blue so that we hope to make plenty of wine, which will be just fine.*

*Mr. de Laudonnière decided fifteen days after the arming of the fort to send two barges to TYMANGOUA and they actually went there on the 15th of this month. [The party was] conducted*

*Coppie d'une lettre venant de la Floride*
(Paris, Norment et Bruneau, 1565). (John Carter Brown Library, Providence, R. I.)

Plan of Fort Caroline, drawn by a settler in 1564, believed to be the first print of any structure erected in the New World by Europeans, and perhaps the first picture drawn in America by a European.

*by Mr. d'Antigny and Captain Vasseur and remained there until the 18th in uncertainty, and upon their return brought very good news saying that they had discovered a gold and silver mine at a place about sixty leagues from our fort, via our River May. When the party arrived there they traded with the Natives who were very scared and always kept on their guard because of their neighbors who were always waging war against them, as they afterwards demonstrated to Mr. d'Antigny and Captain Vasseur.*

*Upon their arrival they left their barges at the water's edge where Mr. d'Antigny ordered some wares left and the barges withdrawn, whereafter the Natives, approaching from their boats where they found the wares, began to reassure themselves making signs as they approached and crying out "AMY THYPOLA PASSON," which means Brother and Friend like the fingers of one hand. When Mr. d'Antigny and Captain Vasseur saw this, they approached and, having been accorded a ceremonious welcome, were led to their village and treated according to their customs, which is, to serve honey and water boiled together with a certain herb which they use and which is very good, And if it please the Lord to let us live another two years, we hope, with the aid which the King will see fit to send, to keep that mine for him.*

*In the meantime, I hope to learn to understand the customs of these Natives who are very good people, making trade with them very easy, showing by signs that they will trade for gold and silver as much as one would trade to them in hatchets, knives, bushhooks, or jewelry of small value.*

*I did not want to forget to write you that yesterday, Friday, we captured a big crocodile, like a lizard but with arms like a human being with joints, and with five fingers on the front paws and four on the back paws, whose skin was sent to France aboard the ships going back home. In that river you see only crocodiles and if one throws in a line in order to fish one catches the most terrible fish one has ever seen.*

*Adieu*

# II

# *Concerning Flying Alligators*

ANOTHER LETTER written shortly after the "Coppie d'une lettre" was authored by Captain Giles de Pysière. He reveals that Moors, savages, and criminals were brought to Florida, and he describes the mutinous activities of the discontented colonists. The author listened to tall tales and reported that flying, man-eating alligators lived in Florida and made other imaginative and exaggerated observations. *Discours de l'enterprise et saccagement que les forsaires de l'isle Floride avoient conclud de faire à leurs capitaines et gouverneurs, estans unis en liberté. Avec la description des bestes sauvages tant marines que terrestres, qui ont estez trouvés dans le circuit de la Floride . . .* par le capitaine Giles de Pysière was published in Paris in 1565. A photographic reproduction of it is in the Library of Congress.

Le Challeux also reported seeing the body of a serpent bearing wings near Fort Caroline (*Last Voyage of Ribaut,* p. 21). He distinguished it from an alligator. Perhaps it was a flying fish.

*Discourse on the Enterprise and Pillage*
*that the Criminals in the Isle of Florida*
*did to their Captains and Governors, after*
*having been freed.*
*With a description of the wild beasts, marine*
*and terrestial, which have been found in the area*
*of Florida.*
*Dedicated to Monsieur the Duke of Bouillon, Great*
*Governor of Normandy*
*By Captain Giles de Pysière,*
*native of the city of Rouen*
*At Paris, for the Pierre de Langre Library*

DEDICATED TO THE DUKE OF BOUILLON BY G. DE P.

*Sir, upon my new state of servitude pledged and dedicated to you alone, all my efforts, weak or strong, are so consecrated to your lordship that anything coming from me would be like coming from you; this book will be very fortunate to be one among those efforts,*

*which virtually escaped from me and was born within a few days in
somewhat imperfect and aborted form while the principal task
which you gave me is waiting to mature. Do not underrate, however, Sir, the present which I am making you thereof, as to one
who is as laden with gold as you may be but, though being so, does
not consider it wrong that I should give riches to the rich, like one
who carries water to the sea though all streams carry it there;
nevertheless, these riches are of such a kind as to burden
you scarcely and as being suitable to be added to your own wealth
invisibly, without appearing to you as any visible increase, as appeared to me as he who passed them on before offering them to
you, without, however, having enriched myself by a single grain of
any kind. Sir, I beg you not to refuse to turn your eye to this distant land, to which one should rightfully think that the noble and
illustrious name of France is known as well as to any other part of
the world.*

*Your humble servant,*
*G. de P.*

### DISCOURSE OF THE VENTURE BY THE CRIMINALS OF THE ISLAND OF FLORIDA AGAINST THEIR CAPTAINS AND GOVERNORS

*Since the time we arrived on the Island of Florida with our
entire company and when we had set free the captives whom we
had taken as prisoners in the environs of said Island, we discovered
a venture which had been undertaken and agreed to by all the
criminals whom we had brought from the Kingdom of France, and
even by foreigners whom we had taken prisoners and to whom we
had granted the right to live in complete freedom and to roam that
land as we had ordered our own criminals to do, except that none
of them was allowed to leave the shores of that land, and this on
pain of death; as to the venture they concluded together, we found
that this had been conducted through the interpreter of a gentleman from among those foreigners, who went out from time to time
in that land to bring in their provisions and necessities according
to their nature. This interpreter was married to a native woman
whom he did not wish to leave nor yet acknowledge for his wife.
Now we proclaimed that these strangers, who are Moors and Savages, should not have anything to do with the women they had with
them, unless they were joined together in good and lawful mar-*

*riage, and that they should abandon their wicked ways on pain of death, for, while they want to live in the greatest lustful abomination ever heard tell of, without God, without faith, without law, it is difficult for them to leave their mistresses and lead a better life, to live as decent people and in the company of Christians. They set out, upon the advice of that interpreter, to poison the companies who held them in such great constraint and who prevented them from leaving this land. Then, on the other hand, the interpreter, who was already acquainted with all of those criminals whom he knew to be living in regret, working hard and having little food, plied them with questions in order to find out, little by little, what they wanted. This sudden questioning was found strange by some who did not want to go along with the scheme in such a short time, not at first thinking it would profit them much. He pursued them to such extent that, by giving them to understand the innumerable ills that might befall them in this place, he easily seduced them by pointing up to them the great freedom which they would have and also the riches afterwards which would be rightfully turned over by the Natives so that they could live as they pleased. They agreed spontaneously and right away wanted to set fire to the powder which had been placed into an underground storage place which we had prepared quickly and above which all of us were sleeping; but none of them thought this to be good because all the merchandise, furniture, and other utensils which we had, would have been lost, and, even if that venture had not been put into effect, and without some of us having noticed anything, they were afraid that this crime would only endanger their lives. They decided among themselves to come to loot us and cut our throats while we would be in our first slumber of the night. However, they encountered one difficulty because of one of the guards, who went along with them everywhere, and whom they had tried to seduce and who, as soon as he found out about their evil intentions, immediately reported it to each of the captains and to their companions so that they would watch out. As soon as the plot became known, there was a remedy and the most apparent villains seized, who, forthwith, finding themselves surprised, confessed their guilt, saying that what they had planned had been due only to the seduction exercised by the interpreter for those Natives, who, as soon as they heard that their plot had been discovered, immediately fled that country; and the next morning punishment was meted out to set an example for the others, and they were chained together again, and they were made to work without ceasing with the laborers who were building in several places in order to fortify the island.*

*Notwithstanding all these adventures, God granted us the power to maintain our stand there and to trust in His mercy.*

*We wanted to send you these things to show that His word has difficulty in taking root in a place so that His glory may be brought to it, but also, that, when it has taken root, it lasts forever.*

THE END

*DESCRIPTION OF THE LAND AND SEA ANIMALS AND MONSTROUS BEASTS ENCOUNTERED ON THE ISLAND OF FLORIDA*

*The author to the Reader:*

*To my reader friend: Among all the books giving spiritual and honest pleasure, none gives me more pleasurable entertainment than those dealing with stories about new lands and the conquest of distant and strange lands, among which is the Island of Florida which has been the latest discovery in the world. Without a doubt it is to be admired over any other place as to singularity and riches because it is full of unknown lands and seas, of strange people, animals, and plants; and the spirit is enriched there by the voluptuous delight of novelty, public opinion is formed and instructed with new knowledge, and the uncertainty of things imagined becomes an assurance by beholding with the eye things as marvelous as prodigious land and sea monsters long ago seen and known in that land of Florida, and there are scattered islands which are something incredible, and where a very big and powerful eagle lives that often comes to refresh itself in a fresh-water river very close to the forest. Then, as soon as it had dipped into the river, it went back to the forest where it was pursued and seized because nets had been spread in several places. Then a lizard was also found there, with the head and neck of a serpent; it also had wings and it flew wherever it perceived some man, or some woman, or a child, and devoured them, and fed them to its young in the forest, so that on the trails one often found half-devoured people who were missing an arm or a leg, the rest having been left on the ground; everyone in the country told us that the lizard was not causing so much trouble at that time, and that they had several times tried to kill it, which they were unable to do. Then we were told how one should get him down. Some thirty men gathered together, all armed with arquebuses, picks, and halberds, to watch it emerge from the woods, in order to kill it, which was done, some of them being ordered to remain on one side, and the others, on the other side. When it emerged from the woods, intent on seizing its prey, it was surrounded on all sides and was killed by shots from the arquebus. Then they went to the place where its young were, who were likewise killed, about which the inhabitants were very happy over being delivered from that evil beast, and thanks was given to God.*

**THE END**

*(Printing completed on July 17, 1565.)*

# III

# *The Sea Hath Nothing Greater*

THE LAST CHAPTER of a beautifully illustrated sixteenth century book (Crispin van de Passe's, *Effigies regum ac principum, eoreum scilicet, quorum vis ac potentia in re nautica, seu marina, prae caeteris spectabilis est* . . . Colonia Agrippina, 1598) has an account of Laudonnière. The picture and inscriptions around it were taken from this book. The account of Laudonnière is a brief summary of his voyage, the colony, the mutineers, and the conquest of Fort Caroline. This Latin work by Van de Passe concludes with the following statement: "The heavens have nothing greater than God, the earth hath nothing greater than Caesar, and the sea hath nothing greater than Neptune and his faithful followers."

*Now let us briefly touch upon the nautical prowess of a certain Frenchman, a noble knight of France. At this time Charles IX was King of France, and as he had been warned by Chastillon [Admiral Gaspard de Coligny] not to postpone too long the sending of reinforcements to the few Frenchmen left by Jean Ribault in Florida, to take care of the King's interests and affairs, Chastillon was given authority to find a man whom he thought could carry out this project. Laudonnière, therefore, was instructed to choose, according to his innate prudence and blameless life, brave, upright, and intelligent men, and since he himself was a very religious man, to choose those whom he would have as associates in taking over this province. He should, after fitting out a fleet, lead it to the New World. Obedient to these things that were said, Laudonnière, having been given full authority to do this thing, leaving the lovely harbor of Porto, set sail for America on April 20, 1564.*

*First they came to the Fortunate Islands or Canaries, then to the Antilles, thereafter to the Island of Santo Domingo. After obtaining fresh water there, but not without the loss of two of their associates, they finally reached Florida on June 22, 1564. This was a very large realm bordering New France, which itself is thought to be equal to Europe in size. Florida is most fertile land, and because of the great number of ships directed to it from various places and at various times, it is very famous.*

*To put it briefly, when Laudonnière had subdued the country-*

Laudibus intactus non Laudonerus abibo?
Florida regnorum comprendit America quæ nunc
Haud minimum cuius Francis virtute subactum.
Perfida quem si non sociorum turpiter hosti
Factio prodisset (cuius tamen, omnibus victis,
Elapsus manibus) quæ, qualia, quanta patrossem!

Crispin van de Passe, *Effigies Regum Ac Principum* (Colonia Agrippina, 1598)

Laudonnière

*side and had performed other great deeds (which this brief report cannot fully discuss, nor was that our intention) he built a well-fortified settlement there. When he thought he had taken care of any possible danger, he was betrayed and seized by his own men; and, banished to the ship, was left to a guard. The leader of this conspiracy was Fourneaux, who incited Marillac to falsely denounce to Laudonnière a certain Gieures, a noble and upright man who, unable to prevent the treachery planned against him, fled into the wilderness. The intimate and close friends of Laudonnière were captured with him, principal of whom were Ottigny and Arlac who were stripped and divested of all their arms and traveling equipment.*

*After these things had been done, our traitors undertook a voyage to New Spain, to do things they had taken into their minds to do. However, Gieures, knowing of the affair, returned to the fortress and freed Laudonnière from captivity. They fortified themselves as best they could, awaiting the arrival of the mutineers. When these did return and found out what had happened in their absence, they feared that they would be punished. Three of the leading mutineers fled, but the rest preferred to take a chance of receiving pardon from Laudonnière and surrendered. He received them kindly but three of the remaining leaders he put to death. The Frenchmen decided to return to their homeland because they were low in provisions. They commenced to destroy their fort, lest an opportunity be given to the Spanish or others to establish themselves there. Finally, unexpectedly circumvented by the Spanish, Laudonnière barely escaped their hands. An entire book of his famous deeds survives, published in Latin, German, and French at Frankfort by de Bry.*

# IV

# *Stranger Things Are Yet to Come*

HENRI LANCELOT VOISIN, Sieur de La Popelinière, *Les Trois Mondes* (Paris, 1582), is a lengthy work on geography and exploration. The three worlds are the Old World (Europe, Asia, and Africa); the New World of North and South America; and Terra Australis, then conceived as a vast area much larger than the Americas. In the second book of this work the author gives special attention to the French activities in Florida. Although the writer's stated purpose is to describe the French expedition of 1565, he first describes the Ribault voyage of 1562 and the experiences of the men left at Charlesfort. He then shifts to Ribault's expedition of 1565 and tells the story of the French commander's arrival at Fort Caroline, Menéndez's conquest of the fort, and the killing of Ribault. The author is overly realistic in his descriptions; he exaggerates and occasionally gives incorrect dates. The section translated was taken from pp. 26 ff. of *Les Trois Mondes*.

*When the Spaniards conquered the Indies they used dogs in hunting down the Indians like beasts. For this purpose the dogs were fed only human flesh cut into sections like chickens and other fowl. The Indians had done the same with Spaniards taken in war. In Florida many events occurred worthy of note, even more so than in discoveries elsewhere.*

*Let us examine now the competency and insufficiency of the French (while bearing in mind the good deeds of the Italian, Portuguese, and Spanish) which might produce, rather than passionate hatred, the courage of our contemporaries and of their leaders to go out on ventures and do better than they had done to date. This is the lesson of the story: the effect and continuation will show you the works and discoveries done by our Frenchmen in the lands known as the West Indies, especially Florida. You can judge whether they were more unfortunate, or less, than the Spanish and English.*

*My purpose is to talk to you about the voyage which the French undertook in 1565 to Florida under the orders of Charles IX. Because they had made the voyage before, I will touch only on the most important things.*

79

*It is natural for all people, not excluding the French, to im-
itate the plans and actions of others. As soon as the discovery of
so many riches and strange lands by the Spanish and Portuguese
was rumored all over Europe, the maritime nations, especially
France, felt piqued into the efforts to do the same in places where
the Spanish and Portuguese had not been. They did not think of
themselves as inferior in navigation or in war or in other pursuits.*

*They were convinced that everything had not yet been dis-
covered, that the world was great enough for men to bring to light
other things even newer and stranger than those already revealed.
Others who were less peaceable fell prey to jealousy such as usually
attends the fortunate outcome of notable enterprises. They were
convinced that, without too many hazards, they could discover and
settle new lands just as the Spaniards had done. Among the first of
the adventurers, one out of two died miserably before they could
peacefully enjoy what they had found. This they felt justified giving to them rights as discoverers. No Prince could declare whether
the natives confirmed the adventurers any rights that they pre-
tended from the King of Spain for having made the first discovery,
or from Pope Alexander VI vesting the same in them. No one had
any right to the property of others! Nor could the discoverer of
Tartarie appropriate it! The Portuguese who were given lands in
the East, as were the Spaniards in the West, did not call themselves
property owners except in certain respects; only for usages in trade
which they maintained there to the exclusion of other nations.*

*Based on these considerations, several French explorations
were undertaken to discover the new world. Some sailed west and
landed in America; others sailed north. Some took the African and
Ethiopian route as I shall describe elsewhere, in order to escape
bad weather and a continuity of misfortune. I shall speak here only
of the people of Dieppe who sailed forth under the Norman Jean
Ribault (redeemed in grace, and appointed by the King under the
maritime laws in 1565) in accordance with his first plan to settle
Florida in 1561.*

*Florida is a coast, a long strip of land on the West Indian
continent with a coastal area curving north. It widens like a sleeve
jutting out 100 leagues into the sea southward, 50 leagues wide. It is
more than 600 leagues from where the True Cross protects New
Spain, on the Gulf of Mexico, away from the coast of Ponet. South
of this is the Isle of Cuba, a good 150 leagues. To the east are the*

*Bahamas and the Lucayes. The tip of this land lies 25 degrees from the North Pole and extends, broadening out slightly, northeastward. Near this cape are very small, low islands, called the Martyrs, along the eastern coast.*

*This is where Ribault landed the first time and was well received by the natives, and where he built a fort which he called Charles-fort. He left 26 soldiers there under the command of Captain Albert, and prepared to go back to France and recruit as many men and women and artisans as he could in order to settle this whole area and to establish there a safe garrison for his nation against any possible attackers. All went well for a while. But finally trouble came because of the punishment of a soldier, whose capture had been ordered by the captain, and the demotion in rank of another whom he had confined on an island three leagues from the fort. They put their chief to death. Then they brought back the banished soldier. They elected Captain Nicolas as their chief, who governed them happily until they tired of having no news from France. They consumed their provisions, resolving to build a boat to return if they did not have relief soon, even though no one knew how to build one. When the boat was finished they asked the natives for rope, which they provided, paying them with knives, bushhooks, mirrors, and such things. Thereafter, looking for resin in the woods, they tapped pines and other sap trees, from which they took enough for caulking. They used a kind of moss with which to stuff the cracks and for caulking. Then they made sails out of their clothing and bedclothes.*

*They set out to sea on the first good wind. The calms and erratic gusts soon held them captive and the fresh water and victuals gave out. Since in three weeks they had advanced only 25 leagues they were restricted to eating not more than twelve grains by weight of corn meal per man per day. But even this gave out, and they devoured their shoes, leather collars, straps, and dried animal skins. Those who tried the sea water suffered with swollen throats and scorched their guts with strange torments. So others drank their own urine. Suddenly, after the vessel's hull burst at the seams, they could not get rid of the water; and, in addition, a huge tidal wave and a gust descended on them with such force that the boat was thrown against a rock; so that because of the waves from above, they could not bail out the water, and even the bravest of them could not encourage the others with the promise of seeing*

land. So for three days they were all in the depths of despair; but
efforts to bail out the water were still to be made. They remained
without food or drink for three days.

Finally, it was suggested that it would be wiser that one die
rather than all of them. The lot fell on the banished Larcher. He
was killed and his flesh was equally divided among them. Then they
drank his warm blood. At last, after being tossed about by the seas,
they saw the land of Britain. This filled them with such joy that
they let the boat drift at the mercy of the waves. An English vessel approached and some recognized that they had water and food.
But the English abandoned the weaker ones and took the rest to
England to their Queen, who was then considering sailing to New
France, to which many voyages had been made by men from Brittany, Normandy and Biscayne.

Laudonnière had gone there [New France] with a troop of
soldiers and remained awaiting the coming of Jean Ribault who
had been commissioned by King Charles, at the recommendation of
French Admiral Gaspard de Coligny, to fit out seven boats with the
rank and authority of lieutenant of the King in those places. He
[Ribault] was expressly ordered not to stop in places where
France was not established—specifically, to avoid the Spanish. In
order to single out the place to go to they [Ribault's forces] were
allowed to go nowhere but Florida. When these orders were di-
vulged, many were found to accompany him on the voyage, motivated however by different desires: some solely to see and explore
the land; others to put to good use their first respite from the civil
wars into which they had been led; and others because of the great
hope of enjoying the prosperity and riches that had been proposed
to them and which Florida promised: complete fulfillment of every
wish that man might desire. Florida is singularly blessed by having
neither the ice and frost of the raw cold of the north, nor the blis-
tering heat of the south. There the fields, without being tended,
produce enough to sustain the life of those who populate it; and require only diligence and industry in order to make it one of the
richest and most productive countries in the world, in view of the
bounty of the land. It has a south-to-north extent of about the size
of Europe and a latitude of 23 degrees. It is swept so often with
the rays of the high sun that it receives abundant warmth, yet tempered not only by the coolness of the night and the dew but also by
generous rainfall. The fertile soil makes the grass green and pushes

the plants to unusual heights. It is rich in gold and animal life. It
has beautiful rivers. Many different trees yield fragrant resins.

As the voyage was delayed four or five months by strong
gales, many volunteers were secured. Since the signing up took
place at Dieppe, to select the most suitable ones, and since they
were paid wages for six months, some who wanted to form an
opinion on such a voyage were startled by the cruel face of the sea
and left without so much as a "goodbye" when they saw that the
time to embark had come. It was in May that 300 men and wom-
en and artisans boarded their ships as the storm blew its worst.
Soon they were at the Isle of Vuich [Wight]. Then on June 14
they set out on the route to Florida, having been on the sea two
months discovering only one of the Antilles, called Lucife at 27
degrees latitude. On August 14 they arrived in Florida, dropping
anchor in the River May. They learned from a Spaniard, who had
been shipwrecked, that some French were more than 50 leagues
away to the north; and on May 23 they took three vessels to la
Carline, which was on the river where Laudonnière was.

This was a comfortable place, not only because of the river on
one side and the forest on the other (a quarter of a league) but
also because of a beautiful plain between the fort and the wood;
and a pleasant hill covered with high and thick greenery through
which they cut a narrow path leading to a spring in the woods.
Having left the provisions and other equipment in the fort, they
reassured their companions, who were concerned about the insufficiency of their provisions. The native men there were handsome,
straight, upright, and sturdy, and had a reddish skin. Each village
had its own King. Their naked skins were marked with strange designs (but the women wore a small piece of animal skin to cover
their feminine parts). Their long hair was carefully arranged on
their heads. There they fastened their quivers, from which they
pulled arrows quickly and skillfully. They are thieves but strictly
honor marriage.

They were waging war against neighboring people of different
languages, with bows and arrows. Their houses are crudely built
like dovecotes made of good-sized trees and covered with palm
leaves. They consider nothing more rich and beautiful than bird
plumes. They live on roots, fruits, green things, and fish, the fat of
which they render into grease and use as butter. As for grain, they
have corn in abundance, seven feet tall and as round as the body of

*a duck, the kernels as large as peas, the ears a foot long and the color of fresh beeswax. They grind and mix the flour to make their "migan" which is like our rice, but does not keep well. They have many wild grapes on vines winding around and in the trees but do not use them for making wine. Their beverage is made from cherry-colored weeds. It makes a strong drink; and in consequence drunkenness must be guarded against. They eat alligators, which have white meat and the same taste as veal.*

*While Ribault was strengthening and defending the fort, five Spanish ships (one of which was between 200 and 300 tons) arrived on September 3 among those who had remained on the coast to guard the ships, calling out that they were enemies. The French set sail but the Spanish did not pursue them and instead went to the River of Dolphins to hide and discuss with the Indians how to defeat the French. Ribault resolved to fight at sea, afraid that otherwise if their vessels were taken they would have no way of getting back to France. So, on September 10, they conferred and encouraged their men, to whom they had added the most skillful of Laudonnière's men; and then they went on to pursue the Spanish. However, the following day the boats were hit by a strange storm which dispersed them until the twenty-third of that month. The Spaniards meanwhile had landed and had won over the Indians to plunder the French of their meager provisions and to seize their other possessions. They found out from the Indians that Laudonnière had in his fort only 200 persons: artisans, women, children and sick people.*

*They made a surprise entry of the fort through an open gate on the 21st of September. They were guided there by the Indians going through strange and swampy woods. They killed the French with their spears while they were sleeping in their beds at dawn; except Laudonnière who, followed by his page boy, leaped over the palisade and saved himself. He left behind him to carry the burden of his faults his soldiers and others who were as lax at their guard as was their chief. Some others escaped the bloody hands of the Spanish (who carried aloft on the points of their halberds and spears the bodies of little children). Those escaping were protected by a Frenchman who guarded the river near the scene of the butchery by the Spanish.*

*The cannon of the fort were trained against these boats, but because of the strong, stormy weather and because the cannon were*

*poorly equipped, they did little damage. Pedro Menéndez sent a
trumpeter as an envoy to persuade those aboard to agree to a settlement or to keep their guns and small boats and withdraw upstream with the other vessels. The response was unenthusiastic. It
was questioned why this was necessary when there was no war between their kings or nations, and since they had been given orders
six months ago by their Prince to make this voyage with the express warning of His Majesty and his Admiral not to touch any
Spanish territory. The French said that if the Spanish wished to
prevent the enjoyment of what the French had discovered and had
settled by the order of their Christian king, they would be found
ready to maintain their advantage.*

*The Spanish were extremely indignant at this and expressed
fear that the French would let their people settle on this land, which
the Spanish claim as a portion of Spanish America, and would from
there prey on the sea routes and revenues of Spain. The Spanish
therefore resolved to do the French as much harm as possible and
to harass them in every way. So, many of them pulled out the eyes
of the dead and exhibited them to the French on the tips of their
daggers; and, committing gruesome barbarity, flicked them into the
water, cursing the French.*

*Jean Ribault, son of the chief, had remained to guard the
boats in the river. Having taken on the escapees from the fort and
not knowing where or how his father was, fearing the worst, he set
out and returned to France with the ship of Mailard on September
25. The boats disappeared from sight quickly. One, after extreme
suffering, arrived at La Rochelle where its needs were cared for.*

*His father, meanwhile, battled the tempest, which had re-
doubled, and was finally wrecked on the coast about 50 leagues below the River May, without meeting the Spanish. So with vessels
wrecked and munitions lost, his men landed except for Captain La
Grange who had placed his faith in the mast which he held tightly,
but in the end he was drowned in the waves.*

*Just as it is true that a trouble doesn't have just one cure, so
it is true that troubles come in bunches. Those who were spared by
the sea were assailed by hunger.*

*They had nothing to eat for eight days, there being no vege-
tation close by which they might eat. The ninth day they found a
boat by which they believed they could reveal their plight to those
at the fort, the distance to which was 12 leagues by land and 50 by*

*sea. They had to cross the River of Dolphins, which is deep and about one-fourth of a league wide, so they caulked the boat with their clothes.*

*As they sent 16 men to the fort for help, they discovered near the fort a company of men in arms, with battle colors flying. These in their extreme distress they recognized as Spanish; Ribault sent an envoy to seek agreement to an honorable settlement. The one called Vallemande [the Spanish leader] protested that he was a gentleman and a soldier and that it was the custom of the Spanish, even toward the French, always to recognize the courtesies of gentlemanly warfare. Then having let Ribault and 30 of his men cross in a boat to the other river bank the Spaniards tied them together in pairs with hands behind their backs. Ribault and Dotigny complained strongly. But Vallemande told them to be patient, telling them this was being done to lead them more safely to the fort where they could be questioned as naval officers, and the others were guarded in order to make use of them. Then about a company of soldiers was deployed against them. These came out with blasts of trumpets, fifes, and drums, and proceeded to administer the swiftest possible strokes of their swords and halberds. So within a half-hour they had won the field by this foul and bloody victory, earning for themselves the badge of dishonor and perfidy. Vallemande broke his promises to Dotigny and Ribault, and they had barely turned their heads to be on their way when they were stabbed in the back with daggers and killed with repeated thrusts.*

*This done, the Spaniards raised up a great bonfire into which they tossed the bodies of the soldiers, women, and children, until they burned to cinders, saying that they were evil heretics who had come to infect the new Christendom with the seeds of their heresies. Then they cut the skin off the face of Ribault and his long beard, his eyes, nose, and ears, and sent the disfigured mask to Peru to exhibit it and guarantee that this had come from Pedro Menéndez and his expedition.*

*Those who returned to France made bitter complaints to the King (under authority of the Admiral) concerning the dishonor bestowed on the King through those who represented His majesty in their careers and about the loss of so many good people and of other things left behind. So, the King, having made complaint to the King of Spain (who disavowed the facts) ordered that enquiries be made in New Spain.*

# V

# *Deposition of Robert Meleneche*

SPANISH OFFICIALS in the New World were painstaking in keeping records. Whenever they captured a foreigner, he was questioned at length and his statements embodied into a formal deposition, usually notarized by a qualified Spaniard. Roberto Meleneche was a seaman and a soldier who sailed with Laudonnière in 1564. The information desired by the Spaniards included descriptions of Florida and the Indians, and the activities of the French in the land claimed by Spain. The account of Meleneche is a valuable source for the activities of the colonists during their first months at Fort Caroline. He stated that Laudonnière was a native of Orleans. A copy of the deposition is in the Woodbury Lowery MSS, Library of Congress, and the original is cited as "Relación del Suceso de la Armada Francesca que fue a poblar la tierra de la Florida" in "Carta escrita al Rey por Juan Rodríguez de Noriega, Sevilla, a 29 de Marzo de 1565," M. S. Direc. de Hidrog., Madrid, Col. Navarette, tomo 14, Doc. No. 33, fols. 3b and 5b.

*Account of the success of the French Armada that went to settle the land of Florida, among which was General Laudonnière, native of Orleans:*

*This account was given by Roberto Meleneche, native of Cruzy, a man who was in the said armada as a militant, who is also a mariner.*

*In the Year of Our Lord 1564, in the Month of March, an armada was ordered in France to colonize the land of Florida. Its sponsor was the Admiral of France, and Cardinal Catillon, his brother. Although at the time the armada was formed, the people said that the King had ordered its formation, with Mr. Laudonnière to be General, and Thomas Basur, a native of Dieppe, Admiral, and Mr. de Otroni, Lieutenant General. The pilots of the armada were French, the chief pilot's name being Tetus, a native of New Harbor [Havre-de-Grâce], another, Miguel Basur, a native of Dieppe, and still another, Gascon, whose last name is unknown. In this armada they brought three ships; the General's ship was a galleon of over 200 tons, although it was not a vessel for mercan-*

*tile traffic because it had been built for war. Another was a 120-ton ship, and still another, an 80-ton ship. Three hundred men went out in this armada, 110 sailors, 120 experienced soldiers, and the rest of them, officers of various rank. Besides these, there were many Africans of unrecorded countries.*

*In this armada, the General's ship carried ten cannon, small and medium-sized; and they carried under the ballast two large guns, medium-sized cannon firing seven-pound balls. They carried in the medium-sized ship four guns; and in the other, smaller one, two. In addition, they carried a large amount of ammunition, pikes arquebuses, armor, gunpowder, bullets, explosive devices, and other things.*

*The said General and Admiral had been militants in the other first armada of 1562, which had gone to Cape St. Helena where a settlement with 30 Frenchmen had been left and of which knowledge had existed before this—about how they had killed their leader and built a small boat in which they left the land and set out for France; that they had killed two of their companions who were eaten by the others, whereby they sustained themselves until they came near the shores of France. There they ran into an English cruiser which captured them because they were at war with them. And the English put them in the dinghy and set them free, and the principals were taken to England aboard the cruiser, and some went to France. Four of these returned to go to Florida in the armada with which we are going to deal.*

*This armada departed from Havre-de-Grâce on April 23, 1564, and on the way they were to reconnoiter the island of Las Palmas in the Canaries, whence they continued their voyage to the West Indies, exploring the island of Dominica, a big island, the first one seen when going to the Indies. They pushed on to the southwestern part of the island, and presently two canoes with Indians approached them and bartered with them pine cones, fowl, and yams, which filled us with wonderment because the Indians of this island are bad folk who never venture out anywhere except for going to war, and they eat human flesh. The Indians came aboard the ships. The next day the armada went to look for water, and 60 Frenchmen went on land, some of whom were interested in the small farms, or fruitful soil of the Indians, and they began to pick fruit, which angered the Natives who started to turn them back and to shoot arrows at them. So the French left to assemble on the*

shore and boarded their vessels and from there fired their arquebuses with which they killed some Indians; and so they left without sustaining any loss save for one man who did not heed the call
to embark, and they did not know whether he was left dead or
alive.

Aboard they would have liked to go back on land to punish
the Natives and recover their man; but the tricky wind convinced
them that they had to leave, and so they set sail and followed the
northern course among all those islands until they came out between Virgin Gorda and Anegada, which are the last two islands,
and from here they kept on going until they came to Florida. The
first land they came to was at 30°, and they went down to 29½°
where they found a river with a mouth as wide as the range of a
culverin shot. Looking for the channel, they found it narrow, and it
was half-way coming from the east, but it was shallow because in
the summer at low tide the stream was only a fathom and a half
deep, and at high tide, two and a half. There are breezes from the
sea every day as there are in Spain, and in the winter the channel
contains one fathom more of water. Entering from the sandbank
to the inside there are many banks, although among them there are
five, six, and seven fathom channels, and it is a good thing that
there are no angry seas. These banks are four or five leagues up
the river, at which point the people of this armada established a
village. From here on up, the river is more soundable and all fresh
water, and so wide in some places that one cannot see across from
one shore to another; and there are countless alligators and Indian
villages on either shore.

The armada came to this country in June and immediately
upon arriving they went to look for people living there, and they
put the smallest of the three ships into the river, which entered the
river without difficulty or damage. They built a fort of timber and
faggots, four or five leagues in the mouth of the river past the
banks mentioned before, inside of which they put their entire con-
tingent, 150 militants, some of them officers, and there were another 50 Africans and other folk, among whom were officers of every
rank, and four French housewives. Into the fort they put eight artillery pieces, the two medium-sized cannon mentioned before, four
medium-sized sacres, two falcons, and eighteen culverins, and great
quantities of all kinds of ammunition which they carried as previously stated.

*Where they built this fort the river is narrow, and they settled there in order to defend the passage with artillery against those who might want to pass ahead; because of this the fort is on the river bank and the range of the artillery easily covers from one bank to the other.*

*After this was done, the other two larger ships were sent back to France to give notice of how and in what state they had remained; and to have 500 more men sent over and other things for which it seemed they should ask. The said ships had been anchored offshore for six weeks after their arrival until they departed on July 22. I feel it is a great stroke of luck that nothing happened to them during all that time inasmuch as they did not have a port. It is believed that by next May they will have returned with the people and all the other things requested.*

*They found all the people of the land peaceful, and learned that there was a chief upstream who was holding three of our men [Spaniards]. They decided to go up the river to see who those men were, and they went up 60 or 70 leagues. Then they discovered that this river is soundable and broad from where they had settled upstream, and that there were villages on both sides of the river, as already reported, and that, at the end of the 60 leagues, he said, it had been learned by signs that the name of the chief with whom the three men were, was Guajaca, and that another's name was Mococo, and that they are powerful and enemies of ours, because, he said, they killed some of the lost ships' crews that had been carried there; and it seemed to them that since they were only a few and that they were tired, they did not dare to go ahead and they went back to the village. It took them ten days to go up those 60 or 70 leagues, and five days for the return trip. He said that the tide goes up the river about 35 or 40 leagues, and from then on, although there was no tide, the water had little current downstream so that they had an easy time navigating. In the summertime, he said, there are many mosquitoes on the banks of the river of the chiefs.*

*He said that all the Natives of this land are good people and have a pleasant disposition. They are not said to eat human flesh; for as observed in the war which they waged against each other, they took captives but did not eat them, although they killed some and made use of others. [He also said] that in this area there is much good maize and many good fish. There is deer; there is wild broomstraw. None of them breed domestic animals, from which it would appear they are lazy people. Many outcasts from the island of Cuba are there.*

*There are large amounts of walnuts and chestnuts. As they do no farming, what they have to eat is poor because it is uncultivated. They have many good grapes, sweet and plump, all of the dark variety. This year, since their arrival, the French have made ten casks or quarts of wine, and they say that the wine came out good and clear. There is an endless variety of trees, cedars, pines, swamp oaks, and live oaks producing acorns which the Indians eat; the timber is the best in the world for making anything they would want. Since their arrival the French have built a very good 18-bench galley boat. The names of the chiefs nearest the settlement are Saturiba, Macani, Carava, and Molua.*

*Eleven men in the village mutinied because, he said, they had been treated badly; and they wanted to row away in the said galley boat, and they took along a small boat, and each of them his arquebus, spade, and shield, and two culverins, together with ammunition therefor, and they left, fleeing from the land, and arrived at the island of Cuba near a small village called Havana; and they took a small boat in which they went to the village and the inhabitants, eight or ten of them, fled, and the French took whatever they wanted and, getting into their boat, left their old boat because it was in worse shape. They took the master of the captured boat and made him take them to the port of Matanzas, and perhaps God wanted them to miss the port and made them go near Havana. There they put into a small port called Arcos and, going on land, searched for water. The ship's master escaped from them and went to Havana and gave notice of what had happened. They armed two boats and sent them out against them and took them and sent three captives to Spain; that is where they are now.*

*This account was taken from one or two of them. The other captives remained prisoners in Havana. These say that the leaders and most of the people who are in the village are ardent Lutherans, and that some are Catholics, although those are in the minority, but they avowed that some of the common people are good Christians. They had been in the country seven months and they say that during the winter they have some terrible days, icy and cold, but that they had not seen snow, and that the land, as far as they could see, is extremely flat; and that they had questioned the Indians as to whether they had knowledge of any mountainous region, and that*

*they said, yes, there is land like that in the interior, and that they*
*also left them, looking for gold which was in that country, and silver*
*and copper; and [Meleneche said] that he saw that some of the*
*Indians were adorned with large discs of the said metals which*
*were suspended from their necks.*

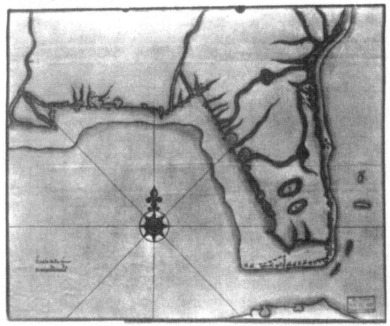

Map Division, Library of Congress

An 18th century Spanish map of Florida, made by Juan de la Puente in
1768, showing the St. Johns River entering Florida's Gulf of Mexico coast to the
southwest of its mouth on the Atlantic Ocean. This water course, which forms a
natural canal across Florida, was described in the 1565 deposition of Robert
Meleneche, and some Spanish, French, and English mapmakers showed this non-
existent canal for the next 200 years. The canal's course is approximately the
same as that upon which the 1964 construction is beginning.

*Giving more detailed information the next day, that French-*
*man said that the river's entrance into the land was to the south-*
*west, more or less. He said further that the chief who had those*
*three men [Spaniards] was said for certain to have killed people*
*from lost ships, because he had come to learn how that Indian,*
*being so far upstream, was able to kill people from lost ships, i. e.,*
*according to the course which the river takes, he must work up the*

*river a short distance from there to the sea, which is near the Tor-
tugas and the Martyrs, as compared with the turn which the land is
making; and it is here where he was able to do what is said of him.
I remember that, carrying in my boat from Havana to Yucatan 70
militants and officers from among those who had been settled in
Polonca, they told me that they had found out from the Indians
that there were villages 30 or 40 leagues inland, and that they
would lead them there, and that they would lead people over the
mountains from place to place so that they would get tired out, and
they would never guide them well, and that they went back. I am
satisfied that these are the same settlements.*

*That Frenchman said that the entire land is flooded because it
is much too low, but that it is a healthful region. I certainly think
that it is much better and more favorable than Cape St. Helena and
surroundings where they had settled first, because it is not so
flooded, although he said that where they settled, they found no
fresh-water river such as this one in that point of land. And if this
were as soundable an entrance as is everything from there on upstream, it would be one of the best rivers in the world.*

*He also said that at Cape St. Helena they did not come across
any rivers worth having, and that, after all, rivers are essential to
a good land and settlements.*

*Asking for information as to whether one would be able to go
from the coast and the mouth of the river to the settlement via the
land route, those Frenchmen said, no, but that a league or a league
and a half below the fort and settlement people could very well be
landed and go to the fort on foot because the forest is not so dense
as to prevent going on foot.*

*This account was taken by me, Juan Rodríguez de Noriega.*

# VI

# *Deposition of Stefano de Rojomonte*

A NATIVE of Paris, Rojomonte sailed with Laudonnière in 1564. Although Rojomonte claimed he sailed away from Fort Caroline with permission of his commander, he was evidently one of the mutineers who attacked Spanish ships and was captured. Spanish officials queried him about rumors of the shipwreck of Juan Menéndez, the son of Pedro Menéndez. The copy of the deposition in the Woodbury Lowery MSS, Library of Congress, is from "Noticia de la población que habian hecho los Franceses a la Florida, 1564," U. S. Arch. Gen. de Indias, Sevilla, Patronato, est. 1., caj. 1, leg. 1/19, ramo 4, p. 1.

*Florida, 1565: News of the settlement which the French had created in Florida. According to the statement made in Cuba by Stefano de Rojomonte, native of Paris. Archives of the Indies, Seville, Simancas, Florida. Discoveries, description and populations of Florida. Patronati - 1. - 1/19.*
*R. 14. -*
*News of the settlement which the French had created in Florida, according to statement made in Cuba by Stefano de Rojomonte, native of Paris.*
*1564 - Florida, Jean Ribault.*
*News from Florida of the settlement and site that the French have created in it, by statement and word of one of those who dwelt there in the Cape regions and of those who came in a sloop to that Cuban shore is the following.*
*Questioned as to what that Frenchman's name was, he said: Stefano de Rojomonte; questioned as to where his place of origin was, he said, Paris.*
*Departed on April 22, 1564, in Armada*
*Questioned as to the boat and Armada in which he departed from France, and at what time and upon whose orders and where he was going to, he said: On April 22, 1564, the Armada in which he came set out upon orders and at the expense of the Queen Mother and of the Admiral and that from the new port three ships had left, one of 300 tons, another of 200 tons, and another of 80 tons and that they had come to settle Florida.*

*Questioned as to who had come as General and what people and artillery they were carrying, he said that the General's name was René de Laudonnière, and that they were carrying 300 men— soldiers and sailors—and that most of the soldiers were gentlemen and important persons and that the Captain was bringing 10 pieces of heavy guns and many other medium-sized ones, and miscellaneous artillery, and many arquebuses, powder, and ammunition, for the Admiral's ship, 12 heavy guns, for the other ship two heavy guns.*

### When they arrived in Florida

*Questioned as to when they had arrived in Florida and within what time and if there were countrymen of theirs in Florida and in what part they were, he said that they had departed from France two months ago, had arrived at the coast of Florida without touching any other land, and had entered a stream which they call the River of May which is, according to what they say, at 31° latitude, and that they jumped on land there and built a fort of earth and faggots so that the ship would be unloaded there, and that in it they had put seven pieces of artillery and the ammunition and provisions and the said person questioned had remained in it with roughly 200 men.*

### Indians and French, enemies

*Questioned as to whether they had friendship, were friends with the Indians, he said that for the first two months after they had arrived in the country they had great friendship with them and the Indians had always brought them fish and many fruits of the soil and they had safely entered and left their villages and homes, and that they had likewise come to the camp of the said French and that the said captain, in order to obtain provisions for himself, had taken all the meal of their harvest and had brought it to the camp because of which, since the Indians had seen it, they had been pursued, and that since then they had been making very cruel warfare, and that a very large number of them had joined together many times to come to fight.*

*Questioned as to whether the ships were in the port to which they had gone, he said that a month after they had arrived at that port, the said captain had dispatched the Captain's and the Admiral's ships to France to give information of the site and the colonization they had done in those parts; so that more people would come over and provisions and other necessaries, that they*

*were waiting for next March; and that the other small ship had
remained in the port and is still there.*

*He was asked if the other ships had carried some gold, silver,
pearls, and other things to France, and he said that the said captain
had found among the Indians a small piece of gold and 12 or 13
pieces of silver and even 50 pearls and had sent all of that to the
said Queen Mother, and that after the said ships had left, the said
French had bought there from the said Indians a quantity of silver
and gold and that all this is in the possession of the captain.*

*Two sloops depart from Florida*

*Questioned as to when and with what ship he had left from
there, and who had come with him, he said that it could have been
more or less two months ago that two sloops which they had there
had departed from the said port of May, that in one of them in
which he had come 36 men and 1 boy had come and that they had
carried two culverins and one cannon and twenty arquebuses and
five pieces of armor, powder, and the necessary ammunition, and
that in the other sloop 25 men and 1 boy had come and that it had
carried two culverins and twenty-five arquebuses, powder, and ammunition for all, and that two days after they had departed a
storm had come upon them and that they were separated and that
they were never again reunited, and that he who is stating this and
the others who had come with him had been on some shoals and
among some islets for fifteen days, that he did not know where they
are, and that from there they had come to Cape St. Nicholas, and
that from that cape to this port near thereto they had taken a small
boat that went to the cape.*

*He was asked if they had left with the permission of the cap-
tain, and he said yes.*

*Questioned as to why and for what they had left there, and
where to and for what they had come, he said that, as the Indians
would not give them provisions as they had used to do and so
caused them to suffer great hunger at the camp, for that reason the
said captain sent the said boats with the said people so that they
would look for provisions and so that they would eat in the meanwhile until help would come from France.*

*Those who fled from Florida*

*Questioned as to whether more than the said boats had left or
had remained, he said that a month ago eleven men had gone into
a small boat and had fled from the said port; that they had de-*

parted from the said port and that since then three other boats had cast for soundings and they were no longer there, and that they had had no further news about them, and that no other boat or ship had departed from those parts, nor had anything similar been done, and that the other sloop which had remained in the said port was going to go to Port Royal where Captain Jean Ribault had made the fort and site on the other voyage so as from there to provide them with the necessaries and to move there in case the Indians would harass them greatly.

He was questioned as to whether Captain Jean Ribault had come in the said Armada; he said, no, because he was in England as a prisoner.

Questioned as to what the 22 Frenchmen who had departed from the said Florida in a boat had done in the said Port Royal where the said Captain Jean Ribault had left them, whether they had gone to France or whether they had come in the Armada, he said that they were in France a month before the said Armada had departed, and that one of them had come in the said Armada and that the others had been taken prisoner on account of the death of Captain Albert, that the said Jean Ribault had abandoned them.

Questioned as to whether they had entered any other port of Florida, he said, no.

Questioned as to whether the port where they are is good and soundable, he said that it is a big river and very soundable within, and that at the mouth there are two fathoms of water and that sometimes the channel expands with the flood season and is soundable.

### The site of the fort

Questioned as to in what parts of the said port the site and fort are established, he said that it may be two leagues from the mouth of the said river, at a high hill, which is above one arm of the said river on the southwest bank.

Questioned as to whether the said French had a language in which to understand the said Indians, he said that they had understood some things because of that interpreter whom the captain had living among the said Indians, and that he did not know whether there was any other language.

Questioned as to whether the said French had had information about the frigate which is somewhere near Havana or about any other island, he said that they had known no more than what the

*said Indians had told them at the Seine [St. Marys River], that it
may have been more or less a year that on the said coast of Florida
three ships of Christians had been lost which had carried much
silver and that the Indians had helped with the landing, and that
three men with boats had escaped who are said to be with the Indians of the province where the boats had been lost, and that some
say that the Christians who are with them are no more and no
fewer, and that they do not know exactly how many there may be.*

*Questioned as to whether, after having taken the boat to that
port, they [the Spaniards] abandoned the small boats which they
had brought, he said that some of the Indians took one of those
boats and were fired upon and sallied forth against by a small dispatch boat, but all the small boats turned to flee on the 28th of
January, 1565.*

*January 28, 1565*

*It is held to be very certain that the boats which the Indians
had said had been lost on the coast of Florida are those of Juan
Menéndez, and that the men who had been among them had done a
great deal to win their friendship, and that it would be easy to find
them because of what these Frenchmen said, i. e., that they were
near Cape Canaveral.*

# Deposition of Jehan Memyn

MEMYN signed as a soldier with one of the lieutenants of Ribault for the voyage to Florida in 1565. His account of the battles and near battles between the Frenchmen and Spaniards is replete with errors. Evidently he was one of the Frenchmen captured by Menéndez, but treated well by the Spaniards. His deposition was printed in Raymond de Bécarie Fourquevaux, *Dépêches de M. de Fourquevaux, ambassadeur du roi Charles IX en Espagne, 1565-1572*, 8 vols. (Paris, E. Leroux, 1896-1904), I, 131. The deposition was translated by Dr. Joseph Brunet of the University of Florida.

### DEPOSITION OF JEHAN MEMYN, SEAMAN
#### 16th October 1566

*On October 16th, 1566, in the presence of Monseigneur de Fourquevaulx, Knight of the Order of the King, his Councillor and Ambassador to Spain.*

*Jehan Memyn, twenty-three to twenty-four years of age, born at La Rochelle, son of Guillaume Memyn citizen of La Rochelle and proprietor of Le Viart, was heard under oath to tell the exact truth.*

*Questioned as to the reason for his presence in Spain, he answered that he had arrived with the fleet of forty-two ships and two caravels that had come from New Spain and other places in the West Indies to the port of San Lucar on the 27th of the month of August just past, having embarked at the port of Santo Domingo on the island of Hispaniola, as prisoner of a Spanish soldier named Herrera, the latter being a native of Palagos, near Seville, they having left Santo Domingo a few days prior to St. John's Day.*

*Questioned as to why he was a prisoner of the said soldier, he answered that three years ago, come next May, Captain Jehan Duboys was recruiting soldiers in the said town of La Rochelle for the purpose of sailing overseas to take food and help to the French who had gone there a year earlier. And he, a young man wishing to see the world, joined the said captain without being a member of his command and embarked upon a reberque which met, at Belle-Isle, the fleet commanded by Captain Jehan Ribault. And their course was by way of the Canaries and the Island of Dominica*

*where they lay at anchor for two weeks to take on water, then to
the island of La Mona and, finally, to Florida, where they arrived
on a Friday with six ships, namely, the Trinité from Dieppe, another named Espaulle de Mothon, the said reberque from La Rochelle of which the said Jehan Duboys was captain. He does not
remember the names of the others. Upon their arrival at the said
Florida, they found there Captain Laudonnière and other Frenchmen at the fort they had built there; to this were carried the supplies they had brought on the said fleet, such as wheat, wines, biscuits, salted meats, and other necessary supplies, as well as artillery
and ammunition for the defense of the said harbor.*

*Questioned as to the number of men there might be on the
said fleet and in the said fort, and as to the names of the commanders, he answered that they were bringing also women and
young men to work the land; between whom and all the soldiers of
the said fleet and of the fort there may have been approximately six
hundred mouths, all told, under the four classifications. The commanders were Jehan Ribault, Loys Ribault, his son, Jehan Duboys,
Gros, Bellot, Martin, Pierre Rennat, and others; and there were also
some gentlemen from Normandy, especially one named Mr. de
Grandpied, who is still alive and a prisoner at Havana; and with
him a boy from Paris, named Jacques, whose father is a domestic
servant of His Lordship, the Cardinal de Bourbon.*

*Asked to recount the event of the capture of the said fort and
the defeat of the said French, he replied that about two weeks after
their said arrival, on a Thursday morning, twenty-five ships were
sighted bearing straight down upon the fort; and having discovered
them, Captain Jehan Ribault sent his son in a lugger to reconnoiter
the said ships and parley with them; and approaching the said ships,
which were Spanish and Portuguese, the men on the twenty-five
ships fired six cannon at the said lugger and refused any other form
of parley. Upon seeing this, the said lugger returned. Then the said
Captain Jehan Ribault and Captain Laudonnière agreed to place
troops on the ship in order to go to see and ascertain the identity
of the said twenty-five ships. And, in truth, the said six ships set
sail to go find the twenty-five ships. These, seeing the said six
French ships bearing down straight upon them, took to their heels
so that they were lost from sight; for they entered a stream fifteen
leagues distant from the said fort. And the said French ships returned to the said harbor of the said fort, where an extremely*

*violent storm blew up. Seeing this, and that the said storm was be-
coming more violent, the said Captain Jehan Ribault disembarked,
accompanied by a number of his men, and went to the fort in boats.
They having arrived there about midnight, the storm increased in
violence so much that the hawsers of the ships at anchor broke.
Four of these broached to and were lost and all the men were
drowned, except three seamen and one cabin boy, all four from
Dieppe; who are alive, prisoners of the Spanish at Havana. The two
other ships in which were the said Captain Laudonnière and the
said Captain Loys Ribault, seeing how violent the storm was,
cleared harbor and put to sea and the said storm lasted two days
and two nights. Meanwhile, the said twenty-five ships, which had
withdrawn into a stream at a distance of fifteen leagues from the
said fort, landed their troops in order to come and catch the said
fort unawares, as they did on the second night of the said storm.
And one of them who spoke French, having advanced, encountered
the sentry as he approached the fort. To him he said that he was
French and while talking to him he killed him. And at once he returned to his companions, all of whom reached the said fort at
about midnight and entered; where they found all the French
asleep, of whom they made a noble slaughter, except for just a very
few. And among these were the deponent and three drummer boys,
one from Dieppe and two from Rouen; and four trumpeters, three
from Normandy and the other from Bordeaux, whose name is
Jacques Dulac. Of the others he does not know the names. They are
still in Florida or on the islands beyond, with the said Pedro Menéndez, these trumpeters who were found on a bed asleep, fully dressed.
As for Jehan Ribault and about sixty others, they were kept under
guard until the next day and then they too were put to the sword;
and they cut off forthwith Captain Jehan Ribault's beard, saying
they wished to send it to the King of Spain. The number of those
who were killed, both in the said fort and on an island nearby might
amount to about three hundred and fifty men.*

*The said Captain Laudonnière, seeing the capture of the said
fort and the defeat of the said French, fled to France with one ship
and one lugger; and the said Captain Loys Ribault withdrew into a
stream thirty leagues distant from the said fort with one ship and
with him about thirty-six men, soldiers and seamen.*

*At the said defeat and shipwreck Captain Jehan Ribault, Jehan
Duboys, Gros, Martin, Rennat and many others, the names of whom*

*he does not remember, died; the women and small children were taken to the island of Porto Rico.*

*He says also that Mr. de Grandpied and about seventeen or eighteen seamen are alive and prisoners at the said Havana.*

*The Portuguese participated in the said defeat as much or more than the Spaniards. And it was the said Portuguese who committed more murders and more cruelties than the said Spaniards. The said fort was burned the next day, with all the supplies it contained.*

*After the said capture of the fort, Menéndez sent two hundred men to a mountain thirty leagues distant from the said fort, and the deponent went in the company of these. On this mountain there is a silver mine. Then, after a fortnight, they took him to Havana; at which place they are building a castle of cut stone which will be very strong when it is finished and is at present not more than six or eight yards high. The said place Havana may consist of about three hundred houses, but is no more than an open village. He says he saw hanging in the said Havana eleven Frenchmen; but could not say for what reason. Then he was taken to Porto Rico, which is a fortified city. To the said place eight French women and four small children had been taken from the said Florida; one of whom was the wife of a Rouen goldsmith and has now married a Portuguese; and afterwards to Santo Domingo, which is a large, fortified city; at which place he was placed on board the said fleet, which has recently arrived in Spain. Two ships of the fleet which had gone with the said Menéndez, laden with sugar and copper, carried fifteen or sixteen French seamen and letters to the said King of Spain; but the privateers seized them near San Lucar.*

# VIII

# *Deposition of Francisco Ruiz Manso*

THE MUTINEERS of Fort Caroline sailed into the Caribbean and in February, 1565, captured a Spanish vessel from Santo Domingo bound for Santiago de Cuba. On board as pilot of the vessel was Francisco Ruiz Manso. He later escaped from his French captors and returned to Spain where he made a deposition. In his statement he described how the French captured the Spanish vessel, pillaged it of its goods, killed a judge and his slave, and made prisoners of the others aboard the ship. These Spanish captives encouraged the Frenchmen to sail to Jamaica where the latter could be captured. A copy of the deposition from the Biblioteca Colombiana, Seville, is in the A. M. Brooks MSS, Library of Congress, and was translated into English by Annie Averette.

*At Seville, on the fourteenth day of the month of September of the year 1565, I, Don Gutiérrez Tello, Treasurer and Judge under Your Majesty for the Contracting Bureau of the Indies, say that inasmuch as a man has arrived here who it is said has come from Havana and who was made a prisoner on the high seas by the French that had sailed from Florida with the intention of capturing or plundering the vessels coming from the Indies and because it is within the province of my services to know and investigate the true facts of the case in order that I may give account of the same to the Royal Council for the Indies under Your Majesty, I therefore placed Martin Ruiz, seaman and a resident of the town of Lepestanto, in this City of Seville under oath and he promised to say the truth in all that he knew and should be interrogated upon and he answered as follows to the questions I propounded to him.*

*Questioned from what parts of the Indies he came and on what ship, he answered that he came from Havana on the ship of which the master is Luis de Palacios and that he arrived at the Port of San Lucar last Monday as a passenger on said ship.*

*Questioned how long since he had left Havana: Answered that the ship on which he had come as a passenger had left Havana about three months ago, more or less.*

103

*Questioned what was the news in Havana in regard to the French who it is said are in Florida and if there were any pirates around those parts: Answered that he knew that some time in the month of February of this year witness sailed from Santo Domingo as pilot on a vessel bound for Santiago de Cuba on board of which there was a Judge of Commissions who had been appointed by the Royal Audiencia of Santo Domingo and sent to the Island of Cuba; that the total number of persons on board were twelve including passengers and crew; that while on their voyage on the sixteenth day of the said month of February, while close to Liburón on a dark night about eleven o'clock more or less, a small dispatch boat manned by oars came alongside of their vessel, while a large ship appeared close by, both vessels being French. As soon as they discovered the vessels were French they tried to escape, but the dispatch boat caught up with them and they commenced fighting and defending themselves. The French killed the Judge of Commissions and a slave belonging to him and wounded witness and four or five others. They then entered our vessel and plundered her of everything she carried; wines, sugar, clothing and slaves; taking the witness and the other men as prisoners. They then transferred them to the large ship where they were placed under decks and where they remained for eight days. By that time the captain and some other Frenchmen spoke to witness and told him that they were part of those that were in Florida and that the Indians there were very friendly to them and that the entrance to the port where they were located was through a river which had a depth of three and a half fathoms at the mouth and very deep inside and that in the said river there was a marsh on which they had built a tower of stone and wood which was very strong and on which they had mounted twenty brass pieces of artillery and it was garrisoned by four hundred men; that they were waiting for ten more ships from France with reinforcements and with women and children to populate the land; that they had sailed from Florida in search of provisions as the men there had nothing to eat and were dying of hunger . . . and that even on that ship they had only stores for two days. They also asked witness if by going into Jamaica it would be possible for them to obtain provisions there, in exchange for the prisoners, including witness, and the clothing they had captured. Witness foreseeing that if the French should enter in Jamaica they would be arrested and he and the other prisoners would gain their liberty, he advised them to go there and they went; but before an-choring they sent ashore two sailors of the prisoners, together with witness and a native of Jamaica, with letters for the Governor and friends they had there.*

*When witness and the others returned on board they brought beef and cassava and other things in order to detain the French in port. They then, not suspecting anything, brought to anchor the large ship, the dispatch boat, and the vessel they had captured from the Spaniards. On the third day about dawn the Governor of the Island, having previously armed and equipped two ships and a frigate, came down on the French ship and commenced firing shot into her. From the first shot they killed two Frenchmen, and in view of this the dispatch boat ran off. The Governor then tried to board the French ship with his frigate, but the French cut the cables and also ran off. But the wind blowing from the sea and the Governor's frigate having oars, she soon caught up with her, in view of which the French Captain called witness, who was below deck, and told him that the Governor had done wrong in not complying with his word. Witness answered him that he knew nothing about it. The French Captain then told witness to make arrangements with the Governor, so that they would be well treated, and that they would surrender themselves. They then surrendered and delivered their arms to witness, and when the Governor came on board he took possession of the ship and arms. After that the Governor held a conference with the officers of his council, to decide what should be done with the French prisoners, and it was decided that they should be kept under arrest and sent to Spain. In this situation witness left them, but as to the dispatch boat (which escaped) witness does not know what became of her.*

*Questioned if the said French ship and dispatch boat were war vessels and if they were well armed, he replied that the ship carries thirty-three men well armed, that the balance of her crew had been transferred to two long boats off the coast of Florida where they say they also have a galleon with oars to patrol that coast. That the dispatch boat had twenty-three men. This is all the witness knows which is the truth, under the oath he has taken, that he is thirty-six years of age, and signed his own name.*

*Questioned what other persons, if any, are there in this city, who may certify to the contents of his deposition or anything else in reference thereto, he answered that in this city there are none*

*that could give any evidence because he is the only one that had
come from that ship.*

FRANCISCO RUIZ MANSO

*By order of the said Señor Juan Gutiérrez Tello, I took this
deposition and delivered it to him this day the twenty-fourth of
September 1565 Francisco Runez Notary Public*

FRANCISCO RUNEZ

# IX

# *The Report of Manrique de Rojas*

RIBAULT'S COLUMNS and settlement at Charlesfort in 1562 threatened Spanish claims to Florida. In 1563 Philip II ordered the governor of Cuba to have the French markers removed and the fort destroyed. In complying with this order, the governor assigned the task to Hernando de Manrique de Rojas who sailed from Havana and explored many of the inlets and rivers along the Florida coast. Manrique was having no success in finding Charlesfort or the marker at Port Royal until he met Guillaume Rouffi. This fifteen-year-old French boy had been left at Charlesfort in 1562 when the other Frenchmen abandoned the settlement. For almost two years Rouffi lived with the Indians. He led Manrique to the ruins of Charlesfort and the stone marker left by Ribault. After destroying these evidences of French occupation, Manrique returned to Cuba, taking Rouffi with him. The report of Manrique and the deposition of Rouffi were translated by the late Lucy L. Wenhold and printed in the *Florida Historical Quarterly* (July, 1959), XXXVIII, 45-62. Her translation is reprinted by permission of the Florida Historical Society.

Rouffi became the interpreter of Menéndez after the capture of Fort Caroline by the Spaniard. In 1566 Menéndez took Rouffi on an exploring venture in the Guale area, north of the St. Marys River. The Spanish command met a party of forty Indians and one Frenchman; the latter had been sent to Fort Caroline after the shipwreck of Ribault in 1565, but on learning the fate of Caroline, had fled north to the Indians rather than attempt to return to Ribault. Menéndez was informed that fifteen other Frenchmen of the Fort Caroline settlement lived in the area for five months before they returned to France. Menéndez was convinced that the lone Frenchman was not only an active enemy against Catholicism among the Indians but had also committed a crime against nature. The Spanish leader used Rouffi to induce the Frenchmen to start toward Santa Elena, the Spanish settlement near the former Charlesfort.

On the journey the Frenchman was murdered by order of Menéndez. Rouffi, however, married the daughter of the Guale chief.

*In the town of San Cristóbal, Havana, on the ninth of July,
1564, after midnight, there entered the harbor of this town the
frigate called La Concepción, in which arrived Hernando Manrique,
formerly captain in Florida. Later, on the tenth of July, before
His Excellency Diego Mazariegos, Governor and Captain General
by appointment of His Majesty, and in the presence of myself,
Francisco Zapata, government scrivener by royal appointment, the
said captain, Hernando Manrique de Rojas, appeared and declared
that he went, by command of His Excellency, to Florida and Point
St. Helena, with a certain expedition, with instructions from His
Excellency and with a royal letter from His Majesty; that he went
and fulfilled his commission and was accordingly reporting to His
Excellency the Governor what he had done. He returned the royal
letter he had received, and delivered a stone marker bearing the
arms of France, the inscription R., and four Arabic numerals. These
things the Governor received in the presence of witnesses.[1]*
*The report made by Hernando Manrique is as follows:[2]*
*Diego Mazariegos, Governor and Captain General by royal
appointment in this Island of Cuba, to you, Hernando Manrique de
Rojas, citizen of this town of San Cristóbal, Havana.[3] Know that
His Majesty has been pleased to state in a royal letter that certain
Frenchmen have established themselves on the coast of Florida and
taken possession there. He desires and commands that I obtain information concerning these persons and what settlement they have
made, according as he directs me in the royal letter, the original of
which you will carry with you. For the fulfillment of His Majesty's
command I have decided to send to Point St. Helena a frigate with
twenty-five men. As the royal service demands for this matter a
qualified person who shall explore the territory and gain information as to what is happening there, I, believing you to be such a*

---

1. *This document is a series of affidavits and a description, but to avoid
repetition and facilitate smooth translations the names of witnesses and formal
certifications of the several scriveners have been omitted wherever possible.*
2. *As is seen, the captain's report is preceded by a reading of the instructions given him by the governor.*
3. *San Cristóbal, usually referred to as a villa but sometimes as a pueblo,
was the governmental center of Havana.*

*person, qualified and trustworthy, who will do in all things what is
most advisable for the service of His Majesty, hereby name and
appoint you captain of the said frigate, of the twenty-five men and
of all others who may go in her or be required for the needs of this
affair. You will go as captain under the flag, commanding and con-
trolling the men, ordering them in whatever may seem to you most
to the service of His Majesty and the success of the expedition,
and punishing the disobedient for whatever offenses they may com-
mit, as is your right. When you shall have embarked in this port,
for the ordering of this expedition and the carrying out of His
Majesty's command you shall keep and follow instructions signed
with my name and countersigned by this present scrivener. In all
respects you will act as becomes a good and loyal captain, and I
will give you full and complete power according as I have it from
His Excellency, with all its incidents and accessories, appurtenances
and rights. If you enter any port of call, whether in this island or in
Hispaniola or elsewhere, I command all justices, knights, gentlemen, officials and good men of the place that they give you favor
and aid and such supplies, men and ships, as you may need. If you
enter ports in the island or Hispaniola or in other parts of these
Indies, I beseech the judges of those towns and ports that of their
grace and in my name, requiring it of them also in the name of His
Majesty, it being a thing so important for the royal service, that
they give you whatever needed assistance you may request. In case
of such necessity you will formalize your request by means of the
royal letter which you carry, leaving a copy of it and keeping with
you your original which was made in the city of Havana on the
twenty-ninth of April, 1564.*

> *Diego Mazariegos.*
> *Francisco Zapata, scrivener, By order of*
> *His Excellency the Governor.*

*That which you, Captain Hernando Manrique, are to do on
this expedition to Point St. Helena and the coast of Florida, of
which expedition I place you in charge, is the following:*

*Having gone out of this harbor, with fortune favoring you
you will enter the Bahama Channel and sail along the Florida coast
until you arrive at the shore of La Cruz, which is in the twenty-
ninth parallel of latitude. There you will land men to seek a stone
column or marker bearing the arms of France, which is set up there.
Having found it you will remove it and destroy it, or, if it proves to*

*be a thing that can be transported in the frigate you will bring it
with you. This is to be done in the presence of witnesses, and of a
scrivener whom you will appoint for this and other necessary
occasions.*

*Then you will continue along the shore of Las Corrientes which
is on the thirtieth parallel and there you will find another of the
same sort.*

*You will proceed thus along the coast until you reach the Saint
Helena River which is in latitude thirty-two. You will enter the river
and attempt to find a wooden fort which is there, and to learn
whether there are any French in it, and if so, their number and
quality, what artillery they have, where they are established,[4] what
are their relations with the Indians, what force they have, and what
preparation will be necessary in order to expel them. If you find the
circumstances such that you can drive them out of the fort you will
do so, bringing to me as prisoners those of them whom you can
capture. You will also bring all the artillery, arms and booty which
you may take from them, razing the fort so completely that no trace
of it shall remain.*

*If by chance you encounter in Florida some captain of His
Majesty with Spanish soldiers who may have gone out for the same
purpose, you will require of him in His Majesty's name and with
the royal letter which you carry that he allow you and your men,
without depriving you of any of the latter, to explore the Florida
coast in order to report to His Majesty concerning it as is his
command.*

*If you should hear that elsewhere there is some enterprise such
as the aforementioned, or should discover a settlement of French
or of any other people who are not vassals of His Majesty, you will
endeavor to reach the place where they are and to acquaint yourself with all the facts, acting in the matter according to the above
directions. In all respects you will act as a good and loyal captain,
with due regard for the royal service and in conformity with the
trust and confidence I place in you.*

*On board the frigate called Nuestra Señora de la Concepción,
at present anchored in the river called Las Corrientes which is in
latitude twenty-seven on this Florida coast, on May 24 of this year
1564, Captain Hernando Manrique de Rojas, commander of the*

---

4. *This seems to refer to a possible settlement aside from the fort.*

*frigate and its men, in the presence of me, Juan Guerra, scrivener
of the frigate, and of other witnesses,[5] declared:*

*That in accordance with the instructions given him by the Governor, after he left the harbor of Havana he came to explore the
coast of Florida in latitude twenty-seven and a half, and proceeded
from that point along the coast to this harbor which is in latitude
twenty-nine, without going more than half a league away from land,
going northward and sailing only by day in order to have a better
view of the coast. The frigate being anchored in the mouth of the
harbor, he ordered Gonzalo Gayon, her pilot, to calculate the latitude. This was done by Gayon and several other persons who had
the necessary knowledge, on the night of last Monday, the twenty-
second of this present month, and they found the latitude to be
twenty-nine. As this is the latitude in which, according to the Governor's instructions, the shore of La Cruz is and where one of the
columns bearing the arms of France should be found, the captain
went ashore to seek it and remove it according to his orders. He
explored the shores of the harbor on the side next to the sea and
on the inner, river sides and went to an Indian village which is
on the bank of one of the rivers. Nowhere did he find the column
nor anything that would appear to have been placed there for that
purpose by the hands of Christians. He communicated with the Indians, but as neither he nor any of his men could understand their
speech he could not learn anything from them about the matter.
As he had been two days in that harbor and wished to go out at
high tide[6] to continue the voyage, in order to put on record the fact
that he had carried out the directions given him he commanded
me, the scrivener, to make an affidavit concerning all the above, I
being one of those who went ashore with him. Even so he commanded me to make a true report of all that might occur in the
harbors into which he might enter, of what he might find there and
what might be done, and to certify it as an eye-witness in order that
His Majesty may be informed of everything. Witnesses being those
aforementioned, he signed: Hernando Manrique de Rojas, before
me, Juan Guerra, scrivener.*

5. *These particular witnesses, whose names are omitted in the translation,
signed practically all the affidavits that make up this narration.*

6. *This is purely a conjectural translation. The word used here is* tiempo
*which means "time" and "weather" and, less frequently, "tide," but the sense
would indicate that the turn of the tide is what is here meant.*

*That same day the captain ordered the anchor weighed, set sail and anchored again somewhat further north. After this, on the twenty-fifth of May, he again ordered the frigate put under sail and ran along the coast until he found a river of some eight or nine leagues from the one mentioned before. He sailed the frigate in and when it was anchored he calculated the latitude and declared it to be twenty-nine and a half. Thereupon he went ashore to some Indians' huts which he saw close to the river mouth, on the arm which is on the north side. Neither in them nor anywhere on the coast thereabout, on river or seashore, did he find Indians or any other people, nor any trace of them, nor did he find any of the French columns. Crossing to the other bank of the river he explored it completely, going more than a league along the other arm which is on the south side, and neither there nor in the other directions in which he explored could he find the column nor anything that appeared made for such use by Christian hands.*

*The same day, having sailed a league further north, the frigate anchored overnight. Next day, the twenty-sixth, we sailed along the coast northward to a river which the captain and Gonzalo Gayon, the pilot of the frigate, said was in latitude thirty. The frigate having run in and anchored in the river, the captain went ashore to an Indian village which is on the arm that runs south. There he found about eighty Indians, and from their signs he learned that there had been on that river three ships of Christians and that these had gone northward to where the point and river of St. Helena are said to be. In one of the huts of the village he found a wooden box with a lid, made by the hands of Christians. The Indians gave it to be understood that this and other things found among them had been given them by bearded men who came in the ships. The captain searched the village and the river banks from one extreme to the other, as also the river mouth, for the French column, but did not find it anywhere.*

*On May twenty-ninth he ordered the frigate's anchor weighed. But as the weather conditions[7] were not good for coastwise sailing he anchored again on the coast a league north of the river just mentioned. In the afternoon of that same day, as he believed the vessels to be in a dangerous position anchored on the coast in the shallows of the river mouth, he ordered her out to sea until the night of the*

7. *Possibly the reference here is again to the tide.*

*next day, May thirtieth, when he again anchored on the coast in latitude which he and Gonzalo Gayon declared to be thirty-two.*

*On May thirty-first he again set sail and entered a river which was said to be the St. Helena. There he and Gonzalo Gayon again calculated the latitude and declared it to be thirty-two.*

*That same day the captain went ashore and found three Indians two of whom came willingly with him to the frigate. From their signs it was learned that ships of Christians had been in the harbor of St. Helena and had gone to an Indian village which, these Indians said, was called Guale, and which is situated on an arm of a river that flows out of another that is north of this harbor. This they indicated by signs and by speaking the name. Then the captain put them ashore and went to the place they indicated, which could be seen from the frigate. On June first, while in this harbor, he took the frigate's boat and went up the arm of the river. He landed near the aforementioned village and went to the micoo,[8] as he is called there. In the house of the micoo and in his possession were found two felt hats of the kind made in Spain, and in possession of other Indians were found other things also from Spain. Speaking by signs with the micoo he learned from him and from the other Indians that the aforementioned ships had been in the harbor and the Christians, whom he described by signs as bearded as we are, had been in the village and had gone away northward up the coast. The captain, with me, the scrivener, searched the entire village and its huts. Neither there nor on the shores of the rivers or the harbor did he find the fort which the Governor, in his instructions, says the French built. Nor did he find any structure at all which could have been built by the French or by any other Christians for that purpose.*

*On the second of June he ordered the frigate sailed out of the arm of the river and anchored at a point in the harbor, above an arm on the southern side, to look for the fort and the French. He landed and explored all the shore from the mouth of the river to the seashore, along the banks and inland, and found nothing.*

*On June third twelve Indians came by land, among them the micoo of their town which is called Yanahume and lies to the south. They gave it to be understood that they wished the captain and the other people to go to their village, and they pointed with their*

8. Micoo, *"chief."*

*hands to show where it was. The captain made signs to the effect
that he would go there at once. He ordered the frigate under way
and anchored above their town, went ashore to it and found neither
French nor fort, nor anything Spanish in the possession of the Indians. From the signs made by the micoo and the other Indians it
was learned that the Christians had gone to the village of Guale and
had not come to this one nor to any other of the seventeen which,
according to the signs they made, are on this harbor.*[9] *They pointed
with their hands to show the directions in which these villages are
located and spoke their names. Other Indians who came in canoes
and by land to see the frigate confirmed by their signs what the
first ones had said. For this reason, and because he could not find
the French nor their fort, the captain declared himself convinced
that there was no French settlement there.*

*On the sixth of June he went ashore and explored the coast
northward for about two leagues, but found neither fort nor French
nor trace of them nor of any other Christians. Then, aboard the
frigate Nuestra, Señora de la Concepción anchored in the harbor,
on the same day, month and year, in the presence of me, the
scrivener, and of witnesses,*[10] *the captain declared:*

*That as he had evidence, furnished both by the testimony of
the Indians of the village called Guale and by the presence among
them of things of Spanish make, that Christian vessels had been in
that harbor and had gone out of it and sailed up the coast; that as
he had obtained the same information from the Indians of the river
which is in latitude thirty, these may be the ships of the French of
whom the governor speaks in his instructions, in spite of the fact
that they have not left the markers on the former harbors nor built
on this one the fort and settlement which the instructions say is in
latitude thirty; that it may be possible that the French left the
markers on his harbor and the Indians have taken them away, or
that the fort and settlement are in some place where it has not been
possible to find them, or that they have been located on another
harbor or other harbors further to the north,*[11] *and that it is proper
for the service of His Majesty to seek them well in order to report*

9. Literally: "are on the bay of this harbor," probably meaning that they
were along the inner shore.

10. Names omitted.

11. Más adelante, literally: "further along," which in this case was certainly
further to the north.

accurately to him concerning the matter. He therefore ordered Gonzalo Gayon, pilot, there present, to weigh anchor as soon as the weather[12] should allow and set sail northward along the coast until he should find another harbor, or harbors, where the French and the fort might be, or where he might obtain more exact information.

On the seventh of June Gonzalo Gayon, as ordered, weighed anchor, went out of the harbor and sailed up the coast to another harbor some three or four leagues further on. He entered it and sailed the frigate along its shores. The captain then ordered Gonzalo Gayon and me, the scrivener, and others, soldiers, to go ashore and look for the French, the fort and the marker. We explored but we found neither these nor any settlement, either of Christians or of Indians.

Smoke[13] was seen inland, apparently at a distance and where the frigate could not sail because of the shallows and flooded land, and thus it was not possible to go there to make inquiries of the Indians.

That same day the captain ordered the frigate out of that harbor and sailing along the coast entered another harbor two leagues further on, where he found neither French nor fort nor Indians nor houses nor any sign of what he sought. Next day he had the anchor weighed and proceeded on his voyage to another harbor two leagues further up the coast. There he disembarked and found traces of Indians in a pine grove which is between two rivers that the harbor has. He found no huts nor Indians, though smoke appeared far inland, and neither fort nor French were found anywhere on the shores of the harbor.

On June the ninth he sailed a league further up the coast and came to two harbors joined in one.[14] He entered with the frigate and went through one of them a distance of about two leagues. Nowhere thereabout did he find the French nor the fort nor Indians nor any settlement except two abandoned houses.

On June tenth he sailed a league further to where appeared

12. Here again the word tiempo is used, but the reference may have been to the tide.

13. The word "smoke" which has no plural in English can be plural in Spanish and is so both here and where used farther on, obviously meaning that the smoke seen was rising from several fires instead of from one.

14. It seems likely that this is the meaning here, though the construction is not very clear.

*two mouths of harbors which are close one to the other.*[15] *Into these he did not enter as it was late and he wished to reach another harbor which was visible further on, and after sailing two or three leagues along the coast he entered harbor* [16] *in which he anchored.*

*On June the eleventh he weighed anchor to go to a river which is on a point on the south side of the harbor.*[17] *As they sailed along, those in the frigate saw a canoe anchored at the point, and immediately two Indians came out of the forest and got into the canoe to go away. The captain ordered Mateo Díaz, master of the frigate, to go to speak with them and to bring them to the frigate if they would come without being made captives or harmed. They came aboard willingly with Mateo Díaz and showed by signs where their village was, on the northwest side of the harbor. The captain took the frigate to that place, and at once other Indians came on board. The captain landed and went to the Indian village. There he found in the possession of the Indians two iron axes, a mirror, some pieces of cloth, small bells, knives and many other things made by the hands of Christians. The Indians explained by signs and some intelligible words that there had been at their village thirty-four men with a ship; that thirty-three of them had gone away and one had remained with them in that land and was now in a village they said was called Usta. They said that they would send for him and he would come the next day when the sun should be high. The captain, having understood, sent two of the Indians to the other village to summon this Christian and gave them a piece of wood with a cross made upon it which they were to give the Christian as proof that there were Christians in the land. The Indian messengers departed at once, and at noon on the twelfth of June there appeared before the captain, in the presence of me, the scrivener, and of witnesses, the said Christian, clothed like the Indians of that country, who declared himself to be a Frenchman.*

*Immediately the captain ordered Mateo Díaz, master of the frigate, to calculate the latitude in order to know the location of the harbor. Mateo Díaz calculated it by the sun, the captain being present, and found it to be thirty-two and a third. Then the captain*

15. *This construction, slightly different from the one above, would seem to intimate mere juxtaposition.*

16. *Whether the one described as visible is not clearly stated.*

17. *The translator concludes that the point was inside the harbor, but it is not specifically so stated. However, the captain must have seen the point from where he was anchored in the harbor.*

*said that inasmuch as it was desirable to find out some things from this Frenchmen in order to know what was to be done in this matter he was giving command that the man be sworn and his deposition taken. He therefore summoned him and called Martin Pérez, one of the frigate's sailors who said he was French, who should translate into Castilian the things the Frenchman might say in his deposition which might not be understood. The two were then put under oath. The Frenchman swore to speak the truth in whatever he knew and might be asked concerning the matter in which they wished him to give evidence, and Martin Pérez swore to translate into Castilian whatever the Frenchman might say that was not understood, without excepting or reserving anything. In acquittal[18] of the oath they said: "Thus I swear" and "Amen!"*

*The Frenchman was asked whether he is a Christian, what is his name and of what country he is a native.[19] He replied that he is a Christian, that his name is Guillaume Rouffi,[20] and that he is a native of Unfein[21] in the kingdom of France. Asked who brought him to these parts he replied that Captain Ribaut did. Asked by the captain from where was this Captain Ribaut, with what ships he came to these parts, what force of men and what artillery he brought, he replied that Captain Jean Ribaut was a native of Dieppe, France, that he came to these parts with two armed galleasses,[22] one of about 160 tons and the other of sixty, a shallop with three lateen sails, and two other, smaller shallops which, at sea, were carried on board the galleasses; that the large galleass carried a hundred men, twenty-five of whom were sailors and seventy-five were arquebusiers, fifteen large brass cannon and two of smaller size and eight brass falcons,[23] besides other arms and ammunition; that the small galleass, captained by the Frenchman Finqueville, carried fifty men, three large guns, one smaller one and six falcons, all of brass, twenty-five arquebuses and other arms and ammunition.*

18. *This is a literal translation, but the translator does not know what is meant.*

19. *This ungrammatical sequence of tenses used in the original has been retained for the sake of its vividness.*

20. *Written* Rufin *in the Spanish original.*

21. *A mis-writing of some name. No such place appears on any map of France. The small town of Envermeu, near Dieppe, is as good a guess as any.*

22. Galazas de armada, *which might mean "navy galleasses."*

23. *The falcon was the light ordnance of the sixteenth and seventeenth centuries.*

*He was asked in what season and from what port they left
France, and he replied that they sailed from New Havre²⁴ in the
kingdom of France on the first day of Lent of the year 1561. Asked
by whose command and at whose cost the expedition had been arranged and what had been its destination, he replied that he understood the expedition to have been made up and sent out at the command and cost of the Queen Mother²⁵ of France, the Admiral²⁶ and
Monsieur de Vendôme, and that each of these gave one thousand
ducats to equip the expedition; that it came directly to this coast
of Florida to settle on the Point and River of St. Helena, and to discover whether it was a good location for going out into the Bahama
Channel to capture the fleets from the Indies. This he knows because he heard it said by everyone and it was common knowledge.*

*He was questioned as to whether they explored any other terri-
tory or harbor of the Indies or any other parts before they arrived
at this coast, and how long they were on the way. He said that after
they left New Havre they neither entered any other harbor nor explored any other territory than this coast of Florida; that he had
heard the pilot call the first land they saw Cape Florida near the
Bahama Channel; that they were two and a half months on the way
from France to this land. Asked whether they met on the ocean
any other ship, he replied that he heard it said that the large galleass, having gotten separated from the small one in which he was,
had met off Bermuda a Spanish vessel which was returning from
the Indies, but that the French captain and his men did not wish
to take the ship nor attack her; that they saw no other ship during
the voyage.*

*He was asked whether any Spaniard came in the galleasses or
whether the people were all French, also whether they were Protes-
tants.²⁷ He replied that the pilot they brought was a Spaniard called
Bartolomé who had with him a son called Bartolomé, and that he
heard it said that they were from Seville; that there was one Englishman and that all the rest were Frenchmen and almost all were
Protestants; that there was one among them who preached the doc-
trines of Luther.*

24. Abranova, *which can scarcely be any other than Le Havre.*
25. *Catherine de Medici.*
26. *Coligny.*
27. Luteranos, *literally "Lutherans"; a term applied by the Spanish indis-
criminately to all Protestant sects.*

*He was questioned as to whether the Frenchmen made a settle-*
*ment or built a fort or set up anywhere any markers bearing the*
*arms of France, and if so, in what places and on what harbors they*
*placed them and where they are; whether there are other French-*
*men besides himself or what has become of the others. He answered*
*that they set up a stone marker bearing the arms of France in the*
*place on the coast where they first explored; that the galleasses*
*entered a harbor three or four leagues south of this one and there*
*set up another marker like the first one, that on a river a little*
*nearer this way, on the same bay, they built an enclosed house of*
*wood and earth covered with straw with a moat[28] around it, with*
*four bastions,[29] and on them two brass falcons and six small iron*
*culverins; that twenty-six men remained in this house and fort and*
*the others returned to France; that Captain Ribaut commanded*
*them to remain there and promised that within six months, for*
*which length of time he left them supplies, he would return from*
*France with more ships and many people, with cattle and other*
*things, to settle that land. They did not set up any more markers,*
*and of the five they brought from France three were taken back in*
*the galleasses.*

*Asked whether he would know how to go where the fort and*
*the markers are and in what latitude they are, he replied that he*
*would know quite well how to go to the fort and to one of the*
*markers, that it was possible to go up the river to them without go-*
*ing out to sea; that he saw the Spanish pilot and two Frenchmen*
*calculate the latitude in the harbor, that the Spaniard said it was*
*thirty-two and a quarter and that the two Frenchmen said it was*
*exactly thirty-two; that the other marker is where he has said, but*
*that he does not know in what latitude it is nor whether he could*
*find the spot unless he could see the river there which he would*
*recognize.*

*Questioned as to whether the twenty-six Frenchmen whom the*
*captain left there are still in the fort, or what has become of them,*
*he said that two of them were drowned in crossing a river in a*
*canoe; that the one who had been left as captain over the others*
*one day struck a soldier with a club, that the soldier drew his sword*
*and in struggling with him killed him; that he and the twenty-two*

28. Cava, *"dug-up earth"*; *probably a dry moat.*
29. *Fort Caroline was triangular; this one seems to have been built on the*
*more usual quadrangular pattern.*

*others who remained, seeing that Captain Jean Ribaut did not come nor did any other Frenchmen, decided to go away to France and for that purpose built a twenty-ton boat near the fort; that when it was finished the Indians of the country gave them a number of ropes made of the strong bark of trees and they rigged the boat with these. The Indians also supplied them with native produce and fed them until they went away in the boat to the province of Guale which is just south of this place. There they were given some native blankets which they made into sails for the boat. Those Indians also gave them supplies. They then returned to this harbor, and the declarant, realizing that there would not be in the boat anyone who understood navigation, was not willing to go with them and remained among the Indians of this section where he has been until now. It is about fourteen months since they went away and no news of them has ever been received.*

*He was asked whether the two falcons and six culverins and the other arms they had were carried away in the ship or were left in the fort or in some other place. He answered that to his knowledge everything was taken away in the boat and nothing at all was left. Questioned with regard to the harbor where they built the fort and where the galleasses entered, whether it is a good harbor with a good entrance, he replied that he knows it to be a very good harbor with a good entrance and five fathoms or more of water in the channel, for he saw it sounded and is himself acquainted with it.*

*He was asked whether the galleasses entered any other harbor of this coast. He answered that they did not, for the shallops, used also for communication with the Indians, were used for sounding the mouths of the harbors further south to see whether there was enough depth for the galleasses which were anchored outside meanwhile; that a harbor with enough water in its channel was never found, or so said those who did the sounding.*

*Asked whether the French took away from this land any silver or pearls or other things, he replied that Captain Jean Ribaut took two or three small pieces of silver that a sailor had gotten in barter among the Indians of the province south of Gaule, that he also took some pearls, deerskins, blankets and other native things; that the twenty-two soldiers who went away in the boat took a hatful of pearls which their captain said he had obtained in trade with the Indians.*

*Questioned as to whether since he had been in this country*

THE SECOND PART—THE DOCUMENTS 121

he had seen or heard it said that there had come any ship or ships, Spanish, French or of any other nation, he answered that he had not seen any ship in this country except those he has described and the one in which he now is. He said that some two months ago, as he was going out in a canoe with some Indians to hunt deer and bears, they went out to a seacoast a league from this harbor and found thick timbers of a ship and rotted fragments of sail and four kegs[30] of the sort that they call corbillon in France and he believes that the vessel was French, both because the French are accustomed to carry in their ships these kegs to take out biscuit and because the arms of France were stamped on them and on one of them was traced with the point of a knife a name, Jean Marin; also because the Indians of the section have told him that some fifteen days before, in a province called Suye which lies some thirty leagues to the north near a large river, they saw two large ships and two small ones out at sea, that one of the small ones, which little vessels the declarant thinks must have been the ships' boats, came to the shore and the Indians fled and would not communicate with those in the boat. That likewise he had heard the Indians say that something like two and half years ago a large ship came to a province on this coast called Amy, which is a little way beyond the province of Suye; that it entered the harbor and the ship's people killed most of the Indians who were there, that very few escaped and fled;[31] that then the ship went away leaving there a fragment of iron cannon. He has not heard from these Indians that any Christians other than those mentioned have come to these parts. He swears to the truth of what he has said and declares himself to be about seventeen years of age. He did not sign the deposition as he says he does not know how to write, and the captain signed it. Some things in the deposition which he, Guillaume Rouffi, did not make clear in Castilian Martín Pérez explained. The latter did not sign as neither does he know how to write. The deposition was read and was certified by Hernando de Rojas before me, Juan Guerra, scrivener.

That same day, on board the frigate, the captain declared that as Guillaume Rouffi was shown to be French and had come with the

30. The word translated "keg" is cesta, "basket," and is followed by the words, de una palla cada una which are probably a reference to size, but the word palla is not in dictionaries. A corbillon used on shipboard is a keg for ship biscuit.
31. The Spanish construction, difficult to render in English, implies that these Indians sought refuge among those who were Guillaume Rouffi's informants.

*other Frenchmen to take possession of this land of Florida, had built a fort and placed there markers bearing the arms of France, he should be held prisoner under close guard on board the frigate and taken to the town of San Cristóbal, Havana, and delivered to the governor to be dealt with as justice might demand. He then ordered that the fort and the markers which the French had built and placed be razed and demolished so that no vestige of them may remain. On June the thirteenth, in the presence of me, the scrivener, he declared that as it seems that the fort and the one marker bearing the arms of France are near this harbor and can be reached by going up the river, and as the tide[32] is contrary and it is not possible to take the frigate there, and as it is proper for him to go in person to remove and destroy the fort and the marker in the presence of a recorder who shall certify the act according to the Governor's orders, he has decided to go up the river in the frigate's boat. He then commanded Gonzalo Gayon, the pilot, that during his absence he, Gonzalo Gayon, was not to allow ashore anyone of those who remained with the frigate, that he was to maintain the usual watches and take all proper precautions for the safety of the frigate and the men in his charge. This command was formally pronounced in the presence of the said Gayon and duly witnessed.*

*That same day the captain embarked in the boat, taking with him me, the scrivener, and other persons from the frigate. Guillaume Rouffi, the Frenchman, led the captain to the place where was the fort[33] the Frenchman built. The place is distant two leagues on an arm of a river on a large harbor, one of two[34] which are close to the southern edge of it. On arrival the captain and the persons with him found a house and fort,[35] which they entered, together with me, the scrivener, and witnesses. In it was found nothing at all. Then the captain commanded that the building be set on fire and burned, and he ordered me, the scrivener, to certify in writing that the house was burned and destroyed. I, the said scrivener, hereby certify and declare that it was burned and destroyed in my presence. Witnesses: Pedro de Torrea, Salinas, Martín Pérez and others.*

---

32. Tiempo *again.*
33. Casa, *"house." There is something faintly derisive in the application of this term to the French structure, which must indeed have been a very flimsy piece of construction.*
34. *Presumably, "two rivers."*
35. *A combination of dwelling and bastioned stockade, one gathers.*

Then the captain went in the boat to another harbor where the stone marker was said to be, to the place where Guillaume Rouffi said it was. It was found on an elevation above an arm of the river of the harbor, somewhat back in the forest. It is of white stone, about the size of a man, and on the upper part of it is inscribed a shield with a crown above it and on the shield three fleurs de lis, and below these the character R. which Guillaume Rouffi says is the name in cipher of the Queen Mother of France whose name, he says, is Catherine.[36] Below this are four Arabic numerals which read 1561. By order of the captain this marker was taken down and thrown to the ground.[37] Thereupon the captain in the presence of me, the scrivener, had the stone marker put into the boat to be taken to the frigate and carried to the Governor at Havana. This was done and witnessed.

On June the fourteenth, on board the frigate, the captain said that as it appeared evident that the French had not made any settlement beyond this harbor and had gone back to France, it was advisable to render to His Majesty prompt account of what has been found on this coast; that since time[38] does not allow of re-exploration of the coast already passed in order to take away the other marker which Guillaume Rouffi says the French set up in the vicinity of the Bahama Channel, because Guillaume Rouffi says he does not know in what latitude it is, that therefore he is commanding Gonzalo Gayon, pilot of the frigate, present, to sail next day for Havana by the best and shortest route; that if before passing the other side of Bahama the wind should again become favorable for long enough to allow of running the Florida coast he should put into harbor to go in search of the marker and do with it as was done with the other one, this being to the royal service.

On June the fifteenth Gonzalo Gayon sailed the frigate out of the harbor and announced his course as via the Lucayas en route for Havana, as the conditions were not favorable for coasting Florida.

36. The character looks more like the letter R than like anything else and can scarcely have had anything to do with the name of Catherine de Medici. Probably it was merely the usual R, the symbol of royalty that stood for Rex or Regina.

37. Throwing the marker on the ground seems superfluous since it was to be taken up again, but doubtless it was a gesture meant to indicate the offense of its presence there.

38. Time or tide or weather. The word is once more tiempo.

*Having inspected these proceedings of Captain Hernando Manrique de Rojas, His Excellency the Governor commanded me, the notary, to make an authorized transcript of them, signed and sealed, to be sent to His Majesty in order that he may know what has been done on this expedition to Florida. Thus he commanded. Witnesses: Juan de Ynestrosa and Antonio de la Torre, residents of this town, before me, Francisco Zapata, notary.*

*This transcript was made from the submitted copy of these affidavits.*

*Nicolas López, secretary of the Royal Camara*
*(with his rubric)*

# X

# *Menéndez and Fort Caroline*

THE ACTIONS of Pedro Menéndez are a major part of the Fort Caroline story. A noble by birth, Menéndez went to sea at the age of fourteen and rose to the rank of captain-general of the Spanish fleet which convoyed merchant ships from the colonies to Spain. He was a man of great ability and unusual honesty; in fact, his honesty was resented by corrupt officials in Spain who succeeded in having him demoted. Menéndez was a loyal servant of the Spanish king and an ardent Catholic. When Philip II offered him the opportunity to rid Florida of the French, the former captain-general eagerly accepted. In addition to serving his country, injuring the Huguenot cause, and restoring his good name, he hoped to find his son whose ships were wrecked somewhere along the coasts of Florida. The decree of Philip II and his instructions, a letter from Menéndez to the king on the dangers of allowing the French to remain in Florida, and the report of Menéndez after the conquest of Fort Caroline are reprinted from A. M. Brooks, *The Unwritten History of St. Augustine,* copied from the Spanish Archives in Seville, Spain, by Miss A. M. Brooks and and translated by Mrs. Annie Averette (St. Augustine, 1909).

### ROYAL DECREE.
### The King.

*To our officers who reside in the City of Seville in charge of the India contracts:*

*I have named the captains, as you will see from the description shown by General Eraso, that they may enlist the 1,400 men who are to go to Florida in the Armada which we have ordered equipped, instructing them immediately upon their arrival what they are to do, and notify me of their safe arrival. You must be immediately notified when the men are gathered together, and as it is expedient with each captain, you are to send a responsible person that he may pay each man one month's salary in advance from the treasury on the day he enlists. It will cost, we suppose, upwards of 11,000 ducats, that they may go provided according to instructions received. You are to give each captain a copy of the*

*order sent, that he may be sure of his men—who, receiving this aid,
neither he nor they be deceived. I also command that according to
these orders you instruct the paymasters so that they may well
understand that each soldier is to have the money in his own hands
so that there be a good understanding between us. This is paid to
them as it will be a long and arduous campaign, and so that they
may work with more zest and the town be established quickly. See
that the captains go at this work with diligence and haste, and you
must immediately see and attend to where you are to lodge these
people and from there embark them. Send with them a person of
trust to guide and lodge them and to see that they are well provided
with food and all necessaries for their money. Keep them well together without disorder or vexation to the people of the land. In-
form me of how you have provided for them and you will have
served me. From BOSQUE DE SEGOVIA
August 15, 1565.*

THE KING.

*To Gen. Pedro Menéndez de Avilés, Knight of the Order of Santi-
ago and our Governor of the Province of Florida:*

*Know—We have understood that from the Kingdoms of
France and England many war vessels have been sent out with a
great number of sailors and soldiers, with intent of going to that
Province, and that now again they are arming and equipping vessels for the same purpose at Havre-de-Grâce and other Ports of
said Kingdoms of France and England. You may do everything to
defend yourselves and capture the Forts they have built and thrust
them from the land, that you may hold it in peace. You might over-
look the damage they have done to navigation. We have arranged
for and ordered 1,500 infantrymen to join you and those you have
with you, and we send them with the fleet and also all the necessaries—and we have provided as Captain-General of the fleet Captain Sancho de Archimiaga, an expert and experienced man of the
sea, ordering him to go to said Province, and in joining you, he
gives you protection by sea as well as by land. Your flag alone must
float, as our Captain-General, and all undertakings must be done
under your flag. And for all enterprises to be undertaken by land
we have appointed a Field Marshal and five Captains to be under
him, and that both they and the infantry are to be directly under
you as our Captain-General and Governor, because this is our will,
and we have expressly ordered it. Your person must be carefully*

guarded. *With your experience both by land and sea we are per-*
*fectly satisfied; still, that you may the better succeed, and that*
*there may be conformity and good will, as it is important, in affairs*
*between you and said Captain Archimiaga and the Field Marshal*
*and the other Captains accompanying him, as they are men of much*
*experience in war, it is our will, and so we order you, that in all*
*things occurring on sea as well as on land concerning the war, you*
*will call these Captains and consult with them, more especially*
*Captain Archimiaga and the Field Marshal—that in this way alone*
*must you decide upon questions of war—because thus it suits us*
*and our service. I trust in them to look into matters and provide*
*all that is deemed advisable in such undertakings—and they will*
*follow and obey you as our Captain-General. Let it be in such a way*
*that there be good will and intelligence between you—no dissen-*
*sions or quarrels, which would be a great drawback, but that you*
*will proceed with mildness and consideration, as I feel assured you*
*will, proceeding to free those lands, and give no quarter to the*
*enemy to take root in them—and if it were possible, and there*
*should be no notable inconvenience, you will divide the fleet. Cap-*
*tain Juan Zurita and his company of Artillery go with the Infantry,*
*as you will see. Of their success you will see to it, and give an*
*account.*

PHILIP II.

*Madrid, September 8th, 1565.*

*To His Catholic Royal Majesty Pedro Menéndez says:*
   *That what he sends Your Majesty is what he declares to know*
*of the coast and lands of Florida, and of the corsairs who it is said*
*have gone to populate it and seize the vessels coming from the*
*Indias, and of the damage they may do, and the remedy to be used*
*in cases where they should have settled. Give them no quarter, and*
*appropriate the coast and lands so that they can be the more easily*
*turned out—that Your Majestry can send to spread the Gospel,*
*prevent the damages that can be done the vessels coming from the*
*Indias is as follows: That while in Sevilla last May, he knew and*
*understood positively from persons coming from the Canary Islands*
*that they had been on the Island of Teneriffe and Port Garachico*
*with a Portuguese named Mimoso, who is a pilot on the run of the*
*Indias, and has a wife and home in France, that he has become a*
*pirate, seizing the vessels of Your Majesty. He carried four men-of-*
*war, and it was said he was going to settle the coast of Florida;*

*that two other large vessels were awaiting him, as soon as he took
on water and provisions in that port, and he saw them [the pirates]
there in a small vessel without disembarking for five or six hours,
where some of the people who wish to be under them came to speak
to them. He then returned to his vessel and set sail to return to the
Indias. Also, that he [Menéndez] heard in Sevilla and in this court
of Your Majesty that the English had gone out with a fleet to the
coast of Florida to settle and to await the vessels from the Indias—
and about a month ago he learned that five large English galleons
with heavy artillery had passed about the end of December along
the coast of Gaul and the tempest had driven them into the harbor
of Ferrol, where they were anchored for a day and a half without
landing, but the fishermen had gone on board to speak to them, and
he says: If the above be true, and the English, French, or any other
nation should feel disposed to go and settle any part of Florida, it
would be very damaging to these kingdoms, because on said coast
of Florida and in said strait of the Bahamas, they could settle and
fortify themselves in such a way, that they could have galleons and
vessels of war to capture the fleets and other private vessels that
came from the Indias, and pass through there, as they would run
great risk of being captured.*

*Also, that if last summer the French and English went to
Florida as we are certain they did, and should have settled and
built a fort in any port, and summered there, giving notice to their
home government as to how they are situated, and should they be
supplied this summer before we can raid upon them, and turn them
out, it would be very difficult to do so on account of the friendship
formed by them with the natives who would help them in such a
way as to cause serious difficulty, and even should we finally succeed the natives would remain our enemies, and this would be extremely disadvantageous. Should they be supplied this summer the
merchantmen which we expect from the Indias would also run great
risk of being captured. Also, that it would be very annoying to have
the above mentioned or others settle in Florida. Considering the
proximity of the Islands of Santo Domingo, Porto Rico, and Cuba,
where there are such vast numbers of Negroes and mulattoes of bad
disposition, there being in each of these islands more than thirty
Negroes to each Christian. And it is a land in which this generation
multiplies with great rapidity. In the power of the French and English, all these slaves would be freed, and to enjoy their freedom*

*would help them even against their own masters and lords and there would be an uprising in the land, and with the help of the Negroes it would be easy to capture us. As an example of this, take Jaques de Soria, France, who in the year fifty-three, with one boat of a hundred tons and eighty men, by simply freeing the Negroes, took and plundered the Islands of Margarita and Santa Marta, and burned Cartagena, plundered Santiago de Cuba and Havana, although at the time there were two hundred Spaniards there. They took the Fort with all it contained, and twelve pieces of bronze artillery and carried them all off. I consider these Negroes a great obstacle to having the French or English settle in Florida or to have them so near; even though they should not be in favor with these two nations, there is danger of an uprising as there are so many cunning and sagacious ones who desire this liberty that I feel sure the design of those who should settle in Florida is to domineer over those islands, and stop the navigation with the Indias, which they can easily do by settling in said Florida. Also he says: That on account of these dangers and many others, it seems to him it would be to the service of God Our Lord, and Your Majesty for the general good of your Kingdoms the Indies, to try and domineer over these lands and coasts, which on account of their position, if other nations should go on settling and making friends with the Indians, it would be difficult to conquer, especially if settled by French and English Lutherans, as they and the Indians having about the same laws, they would be friendly, and being near could rule and each year send out a thousand vessels to easily treat and contract with these lands which are said to be fertile and prolific for sugar plantations, which those nations so much need and are supplied from these Kingdoms. There might also be many cattle good for their tallow and wool and other necessities. What it seems to him that Your Majesty should do in the service of God and Your Majesty's, and for the salvation of so many souls, and the aggrandizement of your kingdoms and your royal estates, is as follows:*

*As there are neither French nor English nor any other nation to disturb them [Spanish settlers], that Your Majesty should send five hundred persons, sailors, laborers, etc., and that among them should be one hundred master carpenters, blacksmiths, plasterers, and builders of mud walls, all with their implements and appurtenances for everything, with their arms of defense, such as arquebuses, cross-bows, etc. That among this number of five hundred people should be four Friars, four teachers, and twelve Christian children, so that the principal Indians would send their children to learn to read and learn the doctrine of Christianity. There should be three surgeons who would go about in small boats, canoes or rowboats with supplies for one year—go straight to Santa Elena and from there find all the paths, rivers and ports most suited and best, by land and water. [One should look to] see the condition of the land for planting and settle two or three towns in the best vicinity, build their fort, to be able to defend themselves against the Indians, that each of these forts should have artillery and ammunition. All this supply with the cost of the voyage will amount to eighty thousand ducats or more. There will be left vessels enough to carry a number of cattle. These [colonists] must be sent from Spain, because in the Indias we could not find suitable vessels nor head workmen of the necessary qualifications and the expedition could not give the desired results, besides the delay would cause much damage. It would be difficult to find the proper kind of people, and even if found the cost would be very much greater, as head workmen gain very large wages in those parts, as do also laborers and sailors. From Havana it would be still more impossible to bring them, as there are none to be obtained, and if they have to settle they must go a long way around, as they cannot enter the mouth of the Bahama Channel, it being as easy and quick to come from Spain as from Havana. It would be important that Your Majesty do this at your own cost and as briefly and with as secret a diligence as possible, and if Your Majesty is not well served in this, find some one in whom Your Majesty can place more confidence, confer with them and let them take charge of affairs—although it would be far better for Your Majesty to do this at your own cost, and with all brevity and secrecy which is the most important thing. Also, he says: That should there be French in this land or on the sea awaiting the merchant vessels from the Indias, it would be necessary to increase this squadron to four more galleons and one thousand men, principally marines—the cost of which for six months would be five hundred thousand ducats more or less.*

PEDRO MENENDEZ.

THE CAPTURE OF FORT CAROLINE AND THE<br>MATANZAS MASSACRE, 1565

*I wrote to Your Majesty from aboard the galleon San Salvador on September 11th, this being the day she left Port. The duplicate of the letter goes in this, and later on I will send the other. While I was on the Bar in a sloop with two small boats with artillery and ammunition there came upon us four French galleons which had run us down with two or three small vessels to prevent us from landing here. Taking the artillery and provisions, although the weather was not propitious for crossing the Bar, I preferred to take the chance rather than surrender myself and one hundred and fifty persons, who were with me, into their power. Our Lord miraculously saved us. The tide was low, there being only one and a half scant fathoms of water on the Bar, and their vessel required one and a half long fathoms. They saw we had escaped them, as they spoke asking me to surrender, to have no fear. They then turned to search for the galleon, thinking we could not escape them. Two days out a heavy storm and tornado overtook them. It seemed to me they could not return to their Fort, running too great a risk of being lost, and to return to capture us they would have to bring a larger force and of the best they had. Thinking that their Fort would remain weak and it was the right time to capture it, I called a council of the captains, who agreed with me, and decided to attack the Fort by land. I therefore took five hundred men, three hundred arquebusiers, the rest pikemen, and with these few, taking our knapsacks and putting in each six pounds of biscuit and a measure of one and a half gallons of wine, with our arms and ammunition; each Captain and soldier—I was among the first setting the example, carrying this food and arms on my back. Not knowing the way, we hoped to get there in two days, it being distant about eight leagues or so, as we were told by two Indians who went with us as guides. Leaving this Fort of St. Augustine in the order above described and with determination on the eighteenth of September, we found the rivers so swollen from the copious rains that it was impossible to ford them and we were obliged to take a circuitous route which had never been used before through swamp and unknown roads to avoid the rivers.*

*After walking until nine or ten o'clock at night, on the morning of the twentieth, which is the feast of San Mateo, we arrived in sight of the Fort. Having offered prayers to the Blessed Lord and His Holy Mother, supplicating them to give us victory over these Lutherans, it was agreed that with twenty ladders, which we carried, we would assail the Fort. His Divine Majesty had mercy upon us and guided us in such a way that without losing one man and with only one injured (who is now well), we took the Fort with all it contained, killing about two hundred and thirty men; the other ten we took as prisoners to the forest. Among them were many noblemen, one who was Governor and Judge, called Monsieur Laudonnier, a relative of the French Admiral, and who had been his steward. This Laudonnier escaped to the woods and was pursued by one of the soldiers who wounded him, and we know not what has become of him, as he and the others escaped by swimming out to two small boats of the three vessels that were opposite the Fort, with about fifty or sixty persons. I sent them a cannonade and call of the trumpet to surrender themselves, vessels, and arms. They refused, so with the artillery found in the Fort we sank one vessel; the others taking up the men went down the river where they had two other vessels anchored laden with provisions, being of the seven sent from France, and which had not yet been unloaded. It did not seem to me right to leave the Fort and pursue them until I had repaired three boats we found in the Fort. The Indians notified them of our actions. As they were so few they took the two best and strongest vessels and sank the other. In three days they had fled. Being informed of this by the Indians, I did not pursue them. Later from the Fort they wrote me that about twenty Frenchmen had appeared in the forest with no clothing but a shirt, and many of them were wounded. It was believed that Monsieur Laudonnier was among them. I have sent word that they make every effort to capture them and bring them to justice. In the Fort were found, among women, creatures, and children under fifteen years of age, about fifty persons. It causes me deep sorrow to see them among my people on account of their horrid religious sect, and I fear our Lord would punish me should I use cruelty with them. Eight or ten of the boys were born here.*

*These French have many friends among the Indians, who show much feeling at their loss, especially for two or three teachers of their hateful doctrine which they taught to the Indian chiefs, who followed them as the Apostles did our Lord. It is a thing of admiration to see how these Lutherans enchanted the poor savage people. I shall use every means to gain the good will of these Indians who were such friends to the French, and there is no reason why I should break with them, and if I can live with them at peace it will be well; they are such traitors, thieves, and drunkards, that it is almost impossible to do so. These chiefs and the Indians, their enemies, all show friendship towards me, which I return and shall continue, unless their depredations increase that I may have to do otherwise.*

*On the 28th of September the Indians notified me that many Frenchmen were about six leagues from here on the coast, that they had lost their vessels and escaped by swimming and in boats. Taking fifty soldiers I was with them next morning at daylight, and, leaving my men in ambush, I took one with me to the banks of the river, because they were on one side and I on the other bank. I spoke to them, told them I was Spanish; they said they were French. They asked me to come over to them either alone or with my partner, the river being narrow. I replied that we did not know how to swim, but that they could safely come to us. They agreed to do so, and sent a man of some intellect, master of a boat, who carefully related to me how they had left their Fort with four galleons and eight small vessels, that each carried twenty-four oars with four hundred picked soldiers and two hundred marines and John Ribault as General and Monsieur LeGrange, who was General of the Infantry, and other good captains, soldiers, and gentlemen, with the intention of finding me on the sea, and if I attempted to land, to land their people on the small boats and capture me. That if they had wanted to land they could easily have done so, but they had not dared and wanted to return to their Fort. That they were overtaken by a hurricane and tempest and were wrecked about twenty or twenty-five leagues from here. That of the four hundred only forty had survived; that the others had perished or were killed by the Indians. That fifty were carried prisoners by the Indians; that John Ribault with his captain were anchored five leagues from there in the swamp without trees, and he had in the vessel with him two hundred persons, more or less, and they believed them to have perished with all the artillery and ammunition, which was a great deal and good. Part of it was with John Ribault and what they had was certainly lost. They were saved, and he asked for himself and companions safe passage to their Fort, since they were not at war with the Spaniards. I then told him how we had taken their Fort and hanged all those we found in it, because they had built it without Your Majesty's permission and because they were scattering the odious Lutheran doctrine in these Provinces, and that I had [to make] war [with] fire and blood, as Governor and Captain-General of these Provinces, against all those who came to sow this hateful*

*doctrine; representing to him that I came by order of Your Maj-*
*esty to place the Gospel in these parts and to enlighten the natives*
*in all that the Holy Church of Rome says and does so as to save*
*their souls. That I would not give them passage; rather would I fol-*
*low them by sea and land until I had taken their lives. He begged*
*to be allowed to go with this embassy and that he would return at*
*night swimming, if I would grant him his life. I did so to show him*
*that I was in earnest and because he would enlighten me on many*
*subjects. Immediately after his return to his companions there came*
*a gentleman, a lieutenant of Monsieur Laudonnier, a man well*
*versed and cunning to tempt me. After much talk he offered to give*
*up their arms if I would grant their lives. I told him he could sur-*
*render the arms and give themselves up to my mercy, that I might*
*do with them that which our Lord ordered. More than this he could*
*not get from me, and that God did not expect more of me. Thus he*
*returned and they came to deliver up their arms. I had their hands*
*tied behind them and had them stabbed to death, leaving only six-*
*teen, twelve being great big men, mariners whom they had stolen,*
*the other four master carpenters and caulkers—people for whom*
*we have much need, and it seemed to me to punish them in this*
*manner would be serving God, our Lord, and Your Majesty. Here-*
*after they will leave us free to plant the Gospel, enlighten the na-*
*tives, and bring them to obedience and submission to Your Maj-*
*esty. The lands being extensive, it will be well to make them work*
*fifty years—besides, a good beginning makes a good end, so I have*
*hopes in our Lord that in all He will grant me prosperity and suc-*
*cess, so that I and my descendants may give to Your Majesty those*
*Kingdoms full and return the people Christians. My particular in-*
*terest as I have written Your Majesty is this: We are gaining great*
*favor with the Indians and will be feared by them, although we*
*make them many gifts.*

*Considering what John Ribault had done, I find that within*
*ten leagues of where he was anchored, three of the vessels of his*
*company were lost; whether they were lost or not, they would have*
*landed the people, unloaded what supplies they could, employed*
*themselves in getting out the brass artillery and the upright posts*
*and tackle, if not lost, of the three vessels, rig themselves as best*
*they could, and if the vessel he was on was not lost he will make*
*every effort to come by sea. Should he do so I await him, and with*
*the help of God, he will be lost. He might also go inland with one*

*of the Casiques, his friend, who lives thirty leagues from here, and is very powerful. Should this be the case I will seek him there, because it is not convenient that he and his companions should remain alive. Should he come by sea to the Fort I have the entrance to the Bar mined with two savage cannon and guns, so that should they succeed in making an entrance, we can sink them. A brigantine is kept in readiness to capture the people and I shall do all in my power to prevent his escape. The things found in the Fort were only four pieces of brass of about five tons, the cannon and guns which had come from France were dismounted and carried to the galleons when they went in search of me. There were found besides twenty-five bronze muskets and as much as twenty tons of powder and ammunition for these pieces, about one hundred and sixty barrels of flour, twenty casks of wine. The balance of the supplies had not been unloaded, as they were hesitating whether they should fortify this Port, fearing I should land here, which I could easily have done. Since their arrival they had spent most of their time in debaucheries over the joy felt at the news they had received that northeast of Santa Elena was a range of mountains coming from the Zacatecas where there were great mines of silver. The Indians from those parts had brought them many pieces of silver to the amount of five and six thousand ducats. We found to the amount of three thousand ducats, more or less, in clothes and all kinds of valuables; some hogs, male and female; also sheep and asses; all this was ransacked by the soldiers; nothing escaped them. Besides the two vessels found in the Port, we found two near the Bar and two others they had stolen from the Indians, loaded with hides. Of these they had drowned the crews and the cargo had been given to an English vessel to carry it and sell it in England or France, and there remained with them two Englishmen. The French had no mariners by whom to [sail] these vessels. These two Englishmen were hanged when the Fort was captured by us. The Englishmen by whom they sent the cargo arrived in port at the Fort we have taken from them, the early part of August of this year, in a galleon of a thousand tons called the Queen of England, with three heavy tiers of artillery; all who saw her wondered and had never seen a vessel so heavily armed that drew so little water; the other three vessels were smaller. It was agreed between the English and French that as the French awaited help from France Monsieur Ludovic [Laudonnière], who was Governor here, should wait for them until the end of September; failing to return, he, Ludovic, was to go to France in search of them, and that by the month of April they would return with a large fleet, to await and capture the fleet of New Spain, which was forced to pass their Fort; that if aid came, for which they had written to France, they would advise the English who would come to this coast by the month of April. It was for this purpose that I found in the Fort a large vessel and seven small ones, and another five, one or two of which had been stolen, and the four they wished to send to France to have them equipped with men and provisions to join the English and themselves by April; that by that time John Ribault would have returned, and with the eight hundred men who remained he wished to go by January to Los Martyres, about twenty-five leagues from Havana, and there built a fort. They had reconnoitered and found it a very desirable port. This was agreed between them, and that before leaving France John Ribault was to obtain the order that they should fortify Los Martyres, a strait by which no vessel could enter or depart without being sighted by them. To keep there always in readiness six vessels, it being the best sea in the world for them. That from there they would take Havana, free all the Negroes; that they would then send to make the same offer to the Spanish of Porto Rico and all other colonies. All this information I gained from the skillful Frenchman to whom I granted life. They had with them six Portuguese pilots whom they hanged when no longer needed; two others had been killed by the Indians, and two were with Ribault. The River San Mateo, running by the Fort we captured, goes seventy leagues inland and turns to the southeast emptying into the bay of Juan Ponce, and from there to New Spain and the port of San Juan de Luca, where there is only upwards of fifty leagues. In the bay of Juan Ponce, they thought next year to build a fort on account of its proximity to New Spain, distant a hundred and fifty leagues and about the same distance from Honduras and as many more from Yucatan, and where with their six vessels they could navigate with ease. On this river are three large Indian towns. The Indians are great friends of the French who have been there three times in search of corn. These French landed there in great need of supplies, having only enough to carry them eight days. Corn they found scarce and took it almost by force. The Indians themselves are great thieves—a poor but brave people. All the Indians are not more friendly to them than to us, and I will not consent to take a grain of corn from*

*them, but prefer to give them of what I may have. I consider this
country so vast and fertile and the danger from enemies and corsairs so great that they can appropriate to themselves the land lying
north of here near New Foundland, of which they are already lords,
and can be sustained by them with ease. Everything should be done
to aid me instead of cutting me off, and Your Majesty must be un-
deceived and know that I am much better able than Your Majesty
to enlarge and aggrandize these your Kingdoms. This Port is 29½
degrees, and the San Mateo which we captured is 31 degrees. The
French and their pilots were mistaken. I have had it taken by the
sun on land. From here to the Cape of Canaveral there are fifty
leagues, three rivers, two ports; between here and Havana, one
hundred miles, more or less, which are navigable in boats among
the keys of Canaveral and Los Martyres, and from there to Havana.
I agree to take the good fieldpieces which we have captured from
the French, and one hundred men [and] go along the borders of
the coast, the boats by sea, anchoring at night near land among the
keys of Canaveral where the sea is as smooth as a river; with the
boats they will be able to discover among the keys the best port and
surroundings to build a fort. So that with the one in Havana and
this one we can at all times guard against the enemy and their
entering to fortify themselves. Nor should we expect fleets or boats
of the Indians. With the people of Havana [and] Santo Domingo,
and Pedro de la Roda, whom I shall have come to my assistance, I
will have until the last of March to build it, then with these vessels
[I will] go over to Havana and seek these people. Having discovered the Port, and on the arrival of Pedro de la Roda in Havana he will find his vessels which I do not propose to take out of
that Port, also his men, so that he may return to Spain as strong as
when he left there. That I shall place one hundred and fifty Spaniards in possession to guard against the Indians who are great war-
riors and whose good will we must gain. Then, by the 1st of April,
I shall return to these two Forts, and in six or eight days I shall
again take to the sea. By the month of March, leaving these two
Forts well equipped and guarded each with three hundred men, I
shall go in vessels that draw little water which I will soon have
here, most of them the ones taken from the French. I will man as
many as I can with five hundred soldiers and one hundred mariners, found a town at Santa Elena, which is fifty leagues from here,
and has within three leagues of it three Ports and rivers, the larg-*

*est of six fathoms of water, the other four fathoms; admirable Ports
and the one we call Santa Elena is the third, the one the French occupied is very small; the three are navigable, one within the other,
so that he who is lord of one is lord of the three. It is the best place
to build a fort leaving three hundred men to finish it, pass on up
the bay to Santa María, which is 36 degrees, one hundred and
thirty leagues beyond Santa Elena; then on to the land of the Indians which is in Mexico, fortify another fort and leave another two
hundred soldiers. This will be the key to all the fortifications of this
country, because from there to the New Land it does not have to be
settled. Inland, about eighty leagues, are to be found a range of
mountains, at their base an arm of the sea which leads to the New
Land. This arm of the sea enters the New Land which is navigable
seventy leagues where there is another sea turning northeast and
we suspect it leads to the South Sea. The Indians send many cattle
from New Spain, which were found on these plains by Francisco
Basques Coronado. They carried the hides to the New Land in canoes to sell to the French in exchange for barter. From here, in the
past two years, they have carried in their fishing boats more than six
thousand hides. The French can go from here in their vessels to the
foot of the mountain range four hundred leagues from the mines of
San Martín and New Galicia and can mine them to their heart's content. It would be well to fix our frontier lines here, gain the waterway of the Bahamas, and work the mines of New Spain. This key
and strength is necessary that Your Majesty should become Lord of
all of it, because by it you will be master of the world. I have written to Pedro del Castillo to send me three hundred soldiers and supplies for eight hundred persons. It would be useless not to have the
three hundred soldiers to serve Your Majesty and to provide the
necessaries. Thus on, from the first of February, Your Majesty can
send a hundred mariners and the equipment and let them bring
everything necessary to found a town in the Bay of Juan Ponce, as
this river is part of San Mateo, which we captured from the enemy.
Eighteen leagues inland from this bay, and from one bay to the
other, we can easily trade with the multitude of Indians that are
there and make them soon learn the Gospel of our Lord Jesus
Christ. In this Bay of Juan Ponce is the Province of Appalache, an
indomitable people with whom the Spaniards have never been able
to treat. Thus will all difficulties be overcome so far as New Galicia
which is about three hundred leagues, and so many more to Vera*

*Cruz, and the same distance to Yucatan. From there this town will be provided with corn, as there is much of it. As we establish the place and build a good City, there will be no need of founding others in Florida. We will then proceed to the New Land, easily work the many mines of silver which are found there, and are the mines of the Zacatecas. In a few years the silver worked from them will support this country and be a treasure to Your Majesty and a suburb of Spain which can be reached in forty days from these Kingdoms. With the scarcity of supplies in the Forts we are suffering much hunger as the grain was burned and so, unless we receive aid soon, we shall suffer terribly. I trust Your Majesty is satisfied that we serve you faithfully and with love and in all truth. Without extending myself further, but promising to keep you advised of all that may happen, may God protect Your Majesty, increasing your royal Catholic personage with greater kingdoms and possessions as Christianity has need of and your servants desire it should be.*

*From these Provinces of Florida from the banks of San Pelayo and Fort of St. Augustine, October 15th, 1565.*

PEDRO MENENDEZ DE AVILES.

*Quot lepores video, metuunt dum plumbea poma'*

An engraving by Heinrich Ulbrech (Bavaria, 1595) of a 16th century soldier with taper burning and ready for firing his piece.

# XI

# *Memoire of the Happy Result*

FRANCISCO LOPEZ DE MENDOZA GRAJALES sailed with Menéndez in 1565 as chaplain of the expedition. The chaplain later wrote an account of Menéndez from the time he sailed from Cadiz, Spain, until he massacred the first group of Frenchmen at Matanzas Inlet on September 29, 1565. Mendoza was a lucid writer and his history is one of the important sources for the founding of St. Augustine and the French-Spanish conflict in Florida. The Mendoza report was translated by Benjamin Franklin French and entitled "Memoire of the Happy Result and Prosperous Voyage of the Fleet Commanded by the Illustrious Captain-General Pedro Menéndez de Avilés. . . ." The translation by French is in a rare book: Benjamin Franklin French (ed.), *Historical Collections of Louisiana and Florida, Including Translations of Original Manuscripts Relating to Their Discovery and Settlement, with Numerous Historical and Biographical Notes* (New York, 1875), pp. 191-234. The translation which follows was made in rough draft by the late Edward W. Lawson of St. Augustine and reworked by the author of this book. It contains some material omitted by the French translation.

*MEMOIRE OF THE HAPPY RESULT AND PROSPEROUS VOYAGE OF THE FLEET COMMANDED BY THE ADELANTADO PEDRO MENENDEZ DE AVILES*
*STATEMENT BY FRANCISCO LOPEZ DE MENDOZA GRAJALES*

*The Armada left the Bay of Cadiz Thursday morning, June 28, 1565, and arrived on the coasts of the Provinces of Florida, August 28, 1565.*

*Sailing with God-given good weather, we recognized and identified the Islands of Lanzarote and Fuerte Ventura within five days after our departure. Then Wednesday, July 4, we arrived at the Canaries, some 250 leagues out of Cadiz. There we stayed for three days, replenishing our water and firewood.*

*Later, on the following Sunday, July 8, under the command of our General, our eight vessels of this Armada went out in search of the Dominican Islands, unconquered islands of the Caribe Indians. By bad luck, the same night we went out from the Canaries, the*

*"Capitana"* [*the Captain General's ship*] *and a smaller vessel were lost from us. We moved along two days searching the sea for them, but we never met. So, the Admiral ordered that we steer directly toward the Dominican Islands where we could rejoin them. On this same lookout the ship of Captain Francisco Sánchez began to leak. They asked for help, but it could not be given them. The pilot tried to bring her alongside of the other vessels until we reached land for repairs, but the Captain and soldiers aboard forced the pilot to go back to land because of their fear of drowning. The pilot could not do that because of the heavy winds, so they agreed to sail southwest looking for land. In this way we left them with great concern about what might befall them.*

*The other five vessels were blessed with good weather by Our Master and His Blessed Mother until Friday, the 20th of said month, when about ten o'clock we had fresh winds and by two o'clock in the morning it had become a hurricane, the most wild and violent that the men had ever seen. The sea was so high it seemed to wish to swallow us up alive. So great was the confusion and fear that the pilot and the rest of us felt that I was impelled to preach to my brothers and companions, reminding them of the love of Jesus and his justice and mercy. That night I did nothing else but receive the confessions of my brothers. Deadly lightning came upon us and the sea flowed through the vessels. There were 120 of us men on deck because there was no habitable spot. There was only one covered spot, protecting our bread and other food, water, and wine.*

*We saw ourselves in such grave danger that we agreed to lighten the vessel by throwing many pipes of water overboard, and the galley with seven stones that we carried to the mills. There was also thrown out most of the ropes and heavy cables we had aboard. With all this effort done, we still did not rise any in the water but kept sinking. The Admiral was determined to throw all the chests to sea, but so great was the protesting outcry from the soldiers that I was almost on my knees pleading that this not be done and that we should place faith in the mercy of God. And he, considering this matter as a good Christian should, showed confidence in God and spared the luggage. When Jesus sent us His light we knew we were saved; and although the tempest of Saturday was just as severe as the night before, the light gave us hope. But when night came again we found ourselves in the same trap, and we thought we were per-*

*ishing. I preached to them all that night and reinforced them in the faith of our Lord. Sunday dawned on us, encouraging us with its light, which perhaps Thy Majesty will understand.*

*The storm kept up all Sunday and until Monday noon, when our Lord, giving mercy to us, halted the winds and the sea and calmed its wrath. At the beginning of the storm the five vessels were sailing together, but darkness and the hurricane separated them so that we did not see each other again until one morning three days later we saw a vessel coming up and recognized it to be one of ours, although at first we feared that it might be French.*

*Our minds were so disturbed and fatigued by what had happened that the pilots did not know how to set our course. In the end, enlightened by the hand of the Holy Spirit, we went West by Southwest and saw the island of Desirade on Sunday, the day of our Lady of the Snows, August 5. Coming up to them we experienced a heavy shower and strong wind from the sea, which pushed us on to the Island of Dominica, land of the Caribe Indians. We came into port Monday night about nine o'clock. The anchorage made, our Captain at once ordered a host of sailors to take jugs to land for water, because we needed it greatly.*

*An Italian boy of mine went out with them, looking for water in the woods. In the bright moonlight he discovered a turtle under a tree, the largest and ugliest ever beheld by man. At the beginning, as she waddled, they took it to be a poisonous reptile that would kill them if it could; and they went running for the sea, where they had the boat. And as they fled, six men of them, they felt they had not done their duty, and each taking his oar and other sticks, they returned to the place where they had seen her, and found it to be, as I have said, a turtle. They vigorously set to turn her belly up with their oars. She started to run them into the sea but could not do it. They captured her and anchored her by a leg, bringing her aboard the vessel. The next day it took 6 men to cut her up. She had in her belly 500 eggs and more, about the same size and shape as hen's eggs, with yolks and whites, except they were round like a ball children play with and of the same size. Its meat and taste are similar to veal, especially when roasted. They live in the sea and go on land to sleep at night. When they are with eggs like this one, they bury their eggs in the sand and cover them with the same, and in due course the growing ones come out and go to sea where they grow up.*

*Later, on Tuesday morning, the Admiral ordered a boat with sailors to land and get water and firewood; and he told me that if I wanted to go ashore I could, but to be careful. Anxious to touch earth, I did not foresee what might occur. I called to my Italian boy and told him to take half a dozen shirts and some other dirty linen, and gave him a little brick of soap so that he could wash them on land. This he did very well and we had 50 jugs filled with very good water found in the woods, and sent them to the boat. While my boy remained with four other men who were washing their clothing, I went toward some rocks jutting out in the sea, collecting for amusement little shellfish that were there in abundance. Raising my eyes, I saw three naked men coming down the ridge of rocks, and as I was in enemy land I was sure they were Caribes. I ran away as fast as I could to where my companions were and made them all come out and each bring a half-dozen stones. We went out toward them, shouting. They shouted that they were of our people. This relieved me a great deal, considering the risk we had run. What had happened was that when I and my companions had landed, the Admiral would not allow anyone else to do that, and as some were so anxious to set foot on land, five soldiers agreed to swim to where I was. From appearances they understood that the ship was close to land but it was much further than it looked and the current was swift. So of the five, two were drowned and three landed on the ridge of rocks where I was. As they came naked, I thought them to be an ambush of Caribe Indians. I made them get more than 100 Peruvian jars of water, and much firewood; and we returned to our ship about four o'clock of the same day. Within an hour the wind freshened and by Wednesday's dawn we were at the Island of Monserrat, 35 leagues from where we started. From the Canaries to the Island of Dominica it is a voyage of about 800 leagues. Farther on are many other islands called The Saints, and another, Guadeloupe, and others, the Virgins. These have the appearance of being more than 200 leagues in circumference. It is a very rough land but is habitable.*

*At noon, Thursday, August 9, we identified the island of San Juan de Puerto Rico and as night had fallen, our pilot ordered sails furled so that we would remain still among the many banks surrounding the island and port. When dawn came, the weather freshened a bit and we gave it the sails. With an agreeable and clear day we arrived at the port of Puerto Rico, Friday the day of the good-*

fortuned Saint Lawrence. About three in the afternoon we entered and within the port we found our Capitana and its smaller companion ship that separated from us earlier. The cries of joy from all sides were inexpressible, praising the Lord for bringing us together again. At once the Captain and the Ensign joined us and we celebrated with them with some preserves and other things I had brought.

The same day the Admiral and I went ashore and visited the General by whom we were warmly received. Since I had not been requested for supper that night, the next day the General asked me to stay in a good house so we could talk together; and I expressed my appreciation. We were in port four days, three days of it pouring rain. On the fifth day, Wednesday, the fifteenth, the day of our Lady, we embarked at ten o'clock. More than 30 men, including three of the seven priests who came, deserted and hid themselves in this settlement. They could not be discovered, dead or alive, which made the General very angry.

I was not less so because it made hard work for me. I was offered a chaplaincy in this port, a peso of alms for each mass I might say, guaranteed for a year. I did not accept because I did not want to be talked about as the others were; and also because it is a settlement where little advancement is probable; and I wanted to see if my work would be rewarded by the Lord in the journey in which I felt I would serve the Lord, and our Lady, His Blessed Mother.

Men are wealthy there, in cattle. There are men who own 20,000 and 30,000 cows, and as many mares worth 120 Spanish reales. The mares are not worth more, for there is nothing in which they can be profitably used unless it be occasionally to draw loads or to produce colts. As to the cattle, only their hides are profitable for they do not do work and have no value for anything else. A hide is valued at 11 or 12 local reales. They tried to persuade me to remain but it cost Lord Valverde, and I, 8 reales there for a half gallon of wine, not very good either. We stocked up with a few delicacies for the voyage, jerked beef and oranges, limes and potatoes and sugar cane. We got a dozen beef tongues with some dried loins. We did this because by the time we arrived there we knew the hungers we suffered at sea.

The hurricane that struck us treated the Capitana very badly, it being near the land when the storm came up, and all had to make *confessions, expecting death momentarily. The wind was so great that it tore out the foremast together with sails and rigging. As it fell into the sea, much of the rigging remained fastened to the moorings and it made them hang over so much on the side that twice the topsail of the mainmast went under water. Also certain parts of the topsides were broken and it also tore off the highest topmast in the vessel. Thinking the ship to be lost and without ability to sail, they let it drift in the waves until God in his mercy brought them to port, where they repaired the ship as well as possible.*

*In this port of San Juan de Puerto Rico the General bought a vessel so that he could carry 50 men the King ordered raised in this island, with more than 24 horses that were bought here. The day we left port the vessel flooded dangerously and they agreed to lighten the vessel of many things so the men could live. Since this made little improvement, they agreed to run it up on the land. There were 23 horses which were thrown into the sea and died, and only one came to Florida alive. This took care of the situation. This same day a large vessel went to look for Santo Domingo and by order of the General to take on 400 men raised there by royal decree, to come speedily to join us.*

*Moreover, before the armadas left Spain three dispatch caravels were sent by royal order, each separately, and they came to Santo Domingo and Havana. His Majesty commanded what they were to do when we arrived. It seems the second caravel, which left with many sealed parchments and letters giving information on what was planned (and being loaded with many other good things), was approached near the island of Mona, land of Santo Domingo, by a French vessel of our neighbors here. They fought until the caravel surrendered and the Frenchmen entered her and took all the papers and read all the advices and orders that were given for the conquest of Florida. They took all the papers and everything else they found and told the caravel's crew to go in good time to Santo Domingo and advise their own people, thinking that they would be in Florida as soon as the caravel could get to Santo Domingo. In this manner they separated.*

*At four o'clock in the afternoon of Friday, August 17, we came in view of the island of Santo Domingo. The General, putting himself in the mercy of God, directed that the Admiral's ship take the Northern course and put into the mouth of a very dangerous channel which up to then had never been navigated. Although the Ad-*

*miral and all of us were apprehensive, we must do the General's bidding. When we entered, the angry sea and heavy waves seemed ready to consume us. The Admiral ordered that I give comfort to the soldiers with prayers and counseling. All that night was dreadful.*

*At dawn on Saturday morning, the 18th, we were reassured. As we proceeded, we found banks in the middle of the sea, where waves broke. The pilots made their soundings, studying the depths required for navigation. In places we found 4 fathoms and in other places less. About two hours before sunset we saw the landmarks of a low uninhabitable island, Aguana. God was pleased to allow us to take the banks and the island by day, so we could guard against danger. It was certainly daylight by permission of our Master and His Blessed Mother. If it had been night we could not have failed being dashed to pieces on them. The danger seen, since none of the pilots knew this area, they agreed to lower sails and heave to by the island so that we would not be lost in traveling at night. When Sunday morning dawned, the 19th, the first ship that set sail was the Admiral's ship, in which I came, because the Captain pilot of this ship knew his business. He drew near the Capitana and found the General and told him that their voyage was already dangerous enough. He, nevertheless, gave orders to proceed, and all the other Captains and pilots did the same. All were apprehensive of the dangers because of the many banks. This same day we saw another low uninhabitable island with many banks around it, named Capuana. God was pleased to let us pass it by day and guarded us from all its dangers. In the late afternoon of the same day the "Almiranta" [the Admiral's ship] pulled along the side of the Capitana, and the Admiral and his pilot spoke plainly with the General, and almost in an ordering manner, that the voyage was not being pursued safely. The General persisted in his opinion and commanded the Captains and pilots that the following night all the vessels should follow the Capitana as a leader and away from the danger of the banks. In view of the concern all had in navigating in unknown places in the dark, all the vessels remained at the stern of the Capitana so that it could assure the safety of the others.*

*At dawn on Monday, the 20th, we were all anchored, for the Capitana anchored about midnight for fear of the banks, and all the other vessels did the same. As soon as it was daylight, we recognized another island at the bow, large but low. From here on the navigation was improved, with few banks, and we were reassured.*

*Yesterday, Sunday morning, a boat arrived from the Capitana with some friends of mine and we learned that the General had chosen eight other captains with their ensigns and sergeants in addition to four others that came from Spain. And each captain has 50 men and certain horsemen to govern the land. We were glad to hear this news.*

*About nine o'clock on Monday the Almiranta drew near the Capitana to salute her, as is customary; and the General commanded that all our soldiers be given their arms to clean them and have them ready. In view of the determination of the General about the method of navigation, it is certain that he understood what was thought, but did not wish to discuss it with others. Your Majesty will remember that when I was in Spain and the Armada was being made up, I went to see the General at the port of Santa Maria and he showed me a letter from my King Philip signed with his name, on which it was said that about May 20 there had been sent out from France seven vessels with 700 men and 200 women. In San Juan de Puerto Rico we found news of how they had taken the dispatch caravel. Observing how the sea had broken our Armada and that there was only to be found in port four vessels of the ten that came out of Cadiz, and another bought there to take horses and people raised in that port, and all ill prepared, he understood, as a man of combat, that the French would be waiting for him in ports further on at Monte Cristo or Havana, or Cape Canaveral (the Cape of Canes), which are all on one coast directly on the road to Florida, especially since the messengers they captured said that we would rendezvous in Havana. Therefore, to evade them on account of the little defense we had after losing our vessels, we decided to go North, which is almost to take a return to Spain, although a different route, and to enter the Bahama Channel by the other side as he did. By this manner he thought to have them to the windward if they were waiting. After I had told this to the Admiral and pilot, they said it was true and that there could not have been any other reason to abandon the proper navigation toward Havana. I understand it, as I have said, just as in the letter he communicated to me in the port.*

*We proceeded by this very dangerous navigation, because of so many banks, and Our Lord was pleased to bring us up safely until Sunday, August 26, when we arrived in sight of two islands, one in front of the other, called the Bahamas. So great were the banks among the islands that waves were breaking in the middle of the sea. The General commanded that all the pilots come up sounding to discover the depths. A vessel that was bought in Puerto Rico was caught this same day in 2½ fathoms of water and I thought she would remain there, but it swung sharply to the windward and from the banks to the course where we were. Our Capitana, being among the largest that are now navigated, found itself that early evening in such shallow water that it bumped three times on the bottom with such great blows that we feared flooding because we knew what it would do below. But as this enterprise is of Jesus Christ and His Blessed Mother, the blows carried her off and 6 fathoms were found and then 10 and 12. In this manner we entered the Bahama Channel this same Sunday, about midnight—although this same day had brought us some calm with heavy showers. God was pleased that as soon as we entered the Channel the weather freshened until about 9 o'clock of the following day, Monday, which gave us calm again. The General seeing that we could not navigate, sent us a boat from the Capitana with a half dozen jugs of wine and other presents. Captain Patiño and Captain Diego de Amaya, the principal pilot, who one morning breakfasted with me there in Jerez, seeing that the boat came, requested the General to allow them to visit me and he gave them permission and they spent a good day with me.*

*At three o'clock on Saturday, the 25th of the month, the General came to our vessel to visit it and to bring artillery for the entrance into Florida. He brought two battering rams and two versos [small cannon]; and their powder and balls; and two lombards. After he had armed the vessel he made a speech setting out what we had to do on arriving at the port where the French would be. Not to be too long in this (which would be interesting to record according to the pros and cons that were expressed) the firm resolution of the General was that, despite the 2,000 Frenchmen being in port, we had to enter by defeating them in combat. I replied to him and charged it to his conscience that he look to the 1,000 souls that he had brought, that he might give a good account of them. From this we passed to other things, which being lengthy, I will leave until we see each other, our Lord and His Blessed Mother being pleased. This same day, Saturday, the argument being over, the General called me and said these words to me: "They have told me that thou hast here a relative of thine." I said to him: "Yes, lord."—"Well if I had known it when I chose captains I would have taken care of him, but I did not know of it until on his part, Diego de Amaya told me of it and now I have provided him the office of Sergeant of the Flagship with Captain Mexica, who is a principal knight. He will have that until something better offers itself." I asked him for his hands that I might kiss them, and called the Lord Valverde so that he might see him and give him thanks and entrust the General with the disposition of his person; for the Lord Valverde, Sergeant and Officer of the King, however established, would profit much from this. If he does well and gives a good account of himself, it is a post from which to rise to captain, which I will see done if I do not die before.*

*Monday, August 27, while we were sailing along and almost at the end of the Bahama Channel, Our Lord showed us a mystery of the sky. It was that at about the ninth hour of the night, a comet came out of the sky, borne almost directly above, but toward the direction of the rising sun and went away giving such a light from itself that it appeared to be like the sun and it went traveling to the West, where Florida is. It lasted about the length of time in which one could recite the Creed twice. We took it for a good sign, according to the custom of the sea.*

*Later Tuesday, the 28th, it dawned with a calm greater than any since the beginning of the voyage. We were a league and a half from the Capitana and the rest. I being weary and tired of reciting and petitioning God and His Mother to remedy the weather, about two in the afternoon, my God provided from His mercy and sent us a good wind. Immediately with full sails we joined the Capitana, and this which I now say I take for a miracle: That when we were in the calm and joined to the other vessels, none of the pilots of the Armada knew where we were (and there were some who said that we were 100 leagues from Florida); and God and the prayers of His Blessed Mother permitted that this same afternoon we recognized land. We drew near to discover what land it was and anchored a league off shore, and this all the rest did also. We found ourselves in Florida not far from our enemies, which was a great consolation and joy to all of us. This night the General ordered all the pilots to the Capitana to discuss their duties.*

*The next day, the 29th, as soon as it was day the Capitana and all the other vessels raised anchor and went along the coast in* search of our enemies or for some good port where the people could disembark.

Thursday, the 30th, we were given a time of head winds which made us throw out the anchor. We were with contrary winds for four days so that we could not navigate further. When these were lacking, calm came to us and stopped us. We were anchored all these days about a league and a half off shore. The Capitana was about a league ahead of us. We could not reach her because of the swift current. Our General, seeing that neither the pilots nor the two French prisoners in our company knew how to reach port by the few land signs (because the coast is so low and level and lacking in signs), decided to put 50 arquebusiers on land. Some captains made many bonfires so that the Indians would come up to see what it was. They are so animal-like they did not care about it and no one came. When our people saw this, they went into the land; and four leagues from there they found a settlement of Indians by whom they were well received. The Indians gave them good food and embraced them and begged for what was brought. The soldiers were so generous that they gave them many things they carried and the Indians gave them two pieces of gold, although of low carat. It showed they had some and were in the habit of giving it in exchange. The Frenchmen with us said they had been in communication with them for some time.

The Indians wished the Christians to remain there that night so they might feast them, but they did not accept because of the need of taking the good news to the General.

Our General, having received the good news, decided at once, Saturday, September 1, to go on land to the Indians; and he carried them many things of linen, and knives and mirrors and other small things of this class to gain their support, and that they might show us where the French port was. One of the Frenchmen, who understood the language, learned that we had left the French behind about five leagues, which is where God brought us when we first saw land. And we learned we did not then find them because we did not then put men on land to reconnoiter it; and that if we struck them at once we would take them unalerted.

Tuesday, September 4, the Armada went out from the spot and turned toward the North along the coast; and later Wednesday afternoon, about two hours before sunset, we had a view of four vessels of the French that were at the mouth of the river. We were *about two leagues apart. The Capitana drew near with its Armada. There were four vessels besides the Capitana. The General spoke with the rest of the Captains and pilots and ordered that the Admiral in his ship and another close in on the French admiral's ship and that the Capitana and another ship close in on the Capitana of France which to my view were two very large ships of great cost. All other vessels put themselves in the best locations to attack, following the lead of the Capitana. But as our General is so prudent and astute in war, they did not shoot or do any harm but went to the French Capitana and anchored about eight paces from her. The rest of the vessels went to the windward near the enemy. At this point it was about two hours before sunset and in all of this not a word was spoken from one side to the other. Never since I was born have I seen such a great silence in people. Our General decided to speak and said these words to the French Capitana which was the one he had closest: "What people?" They replied: "France."— Then, "What do ye in the land of King Philip? Tell me freely and go in good time. If not, look to what you wish and determine to do." They replied and said: "How is the General of the Armada called?" They said to them: "Pedro Menéndez de Avilés." And our General himself demanded in reply that they speak the name of their General, and they said he was called the Great Lord Gasto. During these words the French Capitana dispatched a boat to its Admiral's ship, and he who gave the message gave it so secretly that we did not know the message that he carried; but we understood the reply of the French Admiral who said: "I am the Admiral; but I will die first." The French having finished saying this, they loosened the moorings and left them in the sea and they made sail and went out close to us. Our Admiral's ship, seeing this, struck out across the French Admiral's ship and said to it: "Strike sails for King Philip." The reply given was very coarse. Our Admiral ordered the firing of a half culverin at them and it struck them in the resisting middle flanks and fell to the bottom. We returned to shoot with the same piece another blast which carried off five or six men. But as these devils are so able at sea, we did not capture anyone, neither by these blows nor by others which our Capitana gave them. We could not put any of them on the bottom, but we took from them that night a great boat that they left, which gave us a good profit. All this night our Capitana was giving chase to the French Capitana, and we to the Almiranta.*

*When it dawned on Wednesday morning, the 5th, the tempest was so great that we expected to be flooded. As our vessels were small, we feared to run the course in the sea and we turned toward land, and about a league and a half from land we anchored the three vessels that came. Being upon the moorings, the wind and sea were so strong that we broke one. We petitioned God that the other would hold us, for if it had broken we could not have escaped crashing on the coast and being lost. As our Capitana was so large, we had it at sea to give chase to the adversaries if it could find any. The weather did not give it a chance to return to save us, and we were in danger of these enemies. This same afternoon at sunset we saw a sail coming on the high sea and we took it for our Capitana, a great consolation to us. When it came near, we recognized it to be the French Almiranta which we had treated badly the night before. We thought it would attack us, but it did not dare and anchored about a league from us toward the land. That night the pilots of the two other vessels were even with us. They put themselves in their boat and came to communicate with our Admiral concerning what they must do. The next day in the morning, believing our Capitana to be lost in the storm or at least forced to sea a hundred leagues, we agreed that, it being day, we should raise the anchors and in good order we would reconnoiter a river that was leeward of the French where we could take port and make ourselves a fort to defend ourselves until help came to us.*

*At dawn on Thursday, the 6th, we began to make our course to the ship at anchor. We saw a vessel beginning to appear on the high seas, and thinking it to be ours, we gave land to the French Almiranta. That which came to reconnoiter us we found to be the French Capitana that our Capitana had chased. Seeing ourselves close to the two, we decided to stay behind the Capitana. Because they would not come up to us and they not having the desire that we await them, we went on the lookout for the port and river where Our Lord and His Blessed Mother were pleased that we found our Capitana with another vessel, since among them they had agreed to do the same as we had. The two captains went on land, one the Lord Captain Andrés López Patiño and another the Lord Captain Juan de San Vicente, a great gentleman, and they were very well received by the Indians in a large house of the Chief, close to the river bank. Immediately, Captain Patiño and Captain San Vicente with industry and diligence ordered a ditch and a foss to be made surrounding this house, with much terreplein of earth and fascines, which is the fortification of this land, there being not a stone for a landmark in all of it. We have disembarked 20 guns of bronze, of which the least is 25 quintals.*

*Our fort is about 15 leagues from that of the enemy. So great were the efforts which those two captains made with their industry, and the fingernails of their soldiers, that without having tools, they made a fort to defend themselves in such a manner that when the General disembarked he was astonished at what they had done.*

*Saturday, the eighth of September, the day of the Nativity of our Lady, the General disembarked with many banners displayed and many trumpets and other instruments of war, discharging much artillery. As I was on the land since the day before, I took a cross and went out to receive them with the Psalm "Te Deum laudamus," and the General came directly to the cross with all the rest that came with him, and kneeling on their knees on the earth they kissed the cross. There were a great number of Indians looking at these ceremonies and thus they did all they saw done. On this same day the General took possession of this land for His Majesty and all the Captains swore him to be General of all this land. Having finished doing this, he offered to all the Lord Captains to do for them all that he could do, especially Captain Patiño who had on this journey served Our Lord and his King well. I understand that he should be well rewarded because by means of his good diligence and not sleeping, there has been made a fort with which we defend ourselves until help comes from Santo Domingo and Havana, which we expect within hours.*

*We are now in the fort about 600 fighting men, the French may be as many and a little more. I have advised the General that it is my opinion that he should not attack again this winter, but rehabilitate his people and await the help we expect by hours. He is such a friend of his own opinion that I do not know if he will have it done that way.*

*God and His Blessed Mother made another great miracle for us. After the General disembarked at the fort, he said the next day he could not rest seeing his ships anchored outside the port a league at sea. This was because two of them could not enter the port because of the great banks and he was fearful that the French would come to attack them. As soon as he considered it, he departed for his galleon with 50 men and ordered that one of the three small boats that he had put in the river depart at once to go and bring the provisions and the people from the galley. They brought in the greatest part of the provisions they could and more than 100 men that were in her ready to disembark. They returned on the course to the port, but before they arrived at the bar by half a league, they were becalmed so they could not proceed and they made anchor for the night. As it began to dawn, the pilot of our Chalupa raised anchor to go over the bar because the sea was increasing with strength. Later, when it was day, and they could see, they found at their backs by the stern of one vessel, two French vessels that had come that night to search it out. If the French had attacked at once when they arrived, it would have been a very great capture, because our people were not supplied with arms and were carrying provisions.*

*As our people recognized by daylight that the vessels were French, they put up a prayer to our Lady of Consolation who was in Utrera, asking of her the help of a little wind, because already the French came upon them. It appeared that She herself came to the vessel; and, with the little wind that She stirred, the vessel entered the bar in such a manner that the vessel just finished entering as the French arrived. As there is a bank and the bar is shallow and their vessels great, they could not enter. Our people and provisions entered in safety together with those two vessels. As the day opened, they discovered four other vessels of the same enemies, although somewhat further off, and these were the same that we found in their port the night we arrived upon them. They came supplied with people and artillery and came to attack our galleon and the other vessel, alone and unprotected. For this Our Lord provided two remedies. The first was that the same night, after we put in the provisions and the people without being sensed by the enemies, the galleon and the companion ship that was with her set sail, one returning to Spain and the other going to Havana to bring help, neither being captured. The second (and what gave us the greatest assurance) was that later the next day there came so great a hurricane that the French could not save themselves from destruction by the sea, being close to shore. Our galleon and its companion were not lost because they went out at midnight so that when the storm struck they were more than a dozen leagues at sea with room to maneuver until God provided better weather.*

*Our good General who is so confident in affairs of war and*

*such an enemy of the French, observing the signs I have mentioned,
called his Captains and discussed with them his decision to go with
500 men and attack the French. Although he had dissent from most
of the Captains and from me and the other priest (we being depu-
tized for the councils), he said that he had decided what he had
to do.*

*Sunday, September 16, he departed with 500 men with many
arquebuses and pikes, each one of the soldiers carrying a twelve-
pound sack of bread on his shoulders and a bottle of wine for the
road. They took two Indian chiefs who were great enemies of the
French, so that they might show the way. According to the practice of those Indians and by the signs they made, we understood
that it was five leagues to the fort of the enemies, but on the road
it appeared to be more than fifteen and a very bad road in the
very hot sun. But all have traveled it, according to the letter we
received from the General today, the 19th of said month. In this
he said that the water was at least knee deep and with very thick
growth and that tomorrow at dawn, Thursday the 20th, they plan
to assault the fort of the enemies. His will and zeal are excellent,
but I wish he were more cautious because it would be wiser for
what he undertakes and more to the service of His Majesty.*

*The winds since they departed have been the worst I have ever
seen. I pray that the Divine Majesty will save us as He knows we
have need. Today in the afternoon of Wednesday the 19th we sent
20 men from this fort loaded with provisions of bread and wine
and cheeses, but the water that has soaked them makes it doubtful
that they will be good on arrival at the place where the General and
his army are. I implore God that the General will do well so that
we may exalt His Holy Catholic Faith and destroy the heretics.*

*Today, Saturday the 22nd, in the morning, after saying the
Mass of our Lady, the Admiral permitted, at our petition, that some
sailors might go fishing, it being a fast day. We clergy would eat a
little fish. Arriving at the place where they wished to cast the net,
they saw a man on land and they jumped out onto the land, and as
they went toward him he raised a banner as a sign of peace. Arriving at him, they captured him and he was a Frenchman from our
enemies. They brought him a prisoner to our fort. He was alarmed,
believing that we would hang him and being very tearful and
frightened. I asked him if he were a Catholic. He said yes he was
and said the prayers. Seeing this, I consoled him and told him that*

*if he told the truth in everything, he had nothing to fear. He promised to tell the truth. Asked from where he came and where he went and what he sought, he replied he was of the French at the fort and that his General ordered him with 15 others to enter a frigate 8 days ago to reconnoiter in our port and discover what we did. They in compliance with this came down the coast and, arriving at the mouth of our port, God sent a hurricane and by fleeing from it and from our port they tried to keep themselves at sea but they could not.*

*In this rough sea and furious wind they made it to the mouth of another river four leagues from us on the Southern border. Here their frigate was lost and five were drowned. The next day the Indians came up on them and they fought and killed three with staves. This one and another began to flee through the woods and hid in a hole to escape. Later the next day they decided to return by the sea and putting themselves in the water up to their necks they arrived yesterday, Friday and the day of Saint Matthew, at the mouth of the river. The other companion decided to go by the sea to their port, but since the river is wide and rough where he was, he drowned. He says also that he knows nothing of the rest of his companions, he never saw them again.*

*Immediately we dispatched ten men, soldiers and sailors, to search out the land for the other companions and bring back the frigate, a nice profit.*

*He says that among the people who are in the fort there are 700 people of whom a third or more are Lutherans and that they have two clerics that preach the Lutheran faith to them, that in his camp there are 8 or 10 Spaniards and that three of them were found among the Indians dressed in their skins and tattooed on their bodies like them. They were from a vessel that was lost on this coast, and since for a long time no people came, they remained with the Indians and some married. They say they have a number of cows and sheep and swine to multiply.*

*He says that their Armada arrived not 20 days before ours and that of all the artillery and munitions they brought they have not disembarked more than 200 quintals of sea biscuits and 200 fanegas (a fanega equals 1.60 bushels) of wheat and certain meat and other things. This pleased us, for if God Our Lord gives good success to our General, as I believe He will, all of this will redound to our profit. What pleased us most is that he says they put 200 men*

*in four vessels to search for us and they have not returned and they
must be lost because since they went out they had two tempests,
the greatest I have ever seen. About noon on Saturday, the story of
the Frenchman having been heard as to how the frigate remained
on shore, the Admiral ordered 10 men, soldiers and sailors, to go in
a well-provided boat to where the frigate was, in order to remove it
and bring it back. The command was undertaken. Our ten men,
arriving near the place where the frigate was, were met by a great
number of Indians and fearing that the Indians would shoot them
with arrows, they decided to return, knowing that they were in the
same place where the fifteen Frenchmen were killed by the Indians,
those who had come in the frigate.*

*Monday, the 24th, the Admiral, being annoyed at how the ten
men had returned without the frigate, ordered a boat to be equipped
and took a dozen men and went up the river to discover what was
there, and to see if there was some settlement of Indians there.
Having come out of the mouth of the river where the frigate was
lost, he moved forward until he contacted them. When the Indians
recognized them to be Spaniards, they received him very well and
helped him to take off the frigate. In the morning of Tuesday they
entered the port with her. As soon as I recognized them I ordered
the bells rung and there was much rejoicing in camp. The frigate
is a very profitable aid to our efforts, because it is like a galley of
15 benches and very serviceable.*

*News of great rejoicing, worthy of recording: This came Mon-
day, about an hour after the Admiral's having brought in the captured frigate, we saw a man coming up, shouting loudly. The first
man that went out to him to know the news was I. He embraced me
with great rejoicing, saying: "Victory! Victory! The fort of the
French is now ours." I promised him his blessings and gave them
to him the best I could.*

*I have already noted how our good General determined by
himself, against many opinions to the contrary, to go upon the
French on the border lands with 500 men as he did, and how this
enterprise is of My Lord Jesus Christ and His Blessed Mother. The
Holy Spirit guided our good General so that he should do it for our
salvation with great victory. The Adelantado has been so proud and
diligent in war and has given such a good account of himself in
all the things ordered by His Majesty, that he will do no less in this
enterprise so important to the crown. He has done it with an ardor*

*and diligence unmatched by any earthly Prince. His presence ani-
mated his Captains and soldiers, reinforcing them with his courageous will; so only his words, without the need of other rewards,
were sufficient to make each soldier fight like a Roman. That this
victory may be better appreciated, I want to give an account of
some of the conduct of this journey. It is understood that only Our
Master and His Mother made possible this journey, without the
force of men, against those enemies of their Holy Catholic Faith.*

*On the 16th of September our good General went out with 500
men, arquebusiers and pikemen; two Indian chiefs went to show
the way to the enemy fort. They were on the road for three days
before arriving there, going in water up to their chests and swimming there on the way. Those who knew how to swim passed in
front and stuck out their pikes and brought the others through the
water after them. In this manner they went on until Wednesday
night, the 18th, when they arrived about a quarter of a league from
the fort of the enemy. They were all that night in that swamp. By
the time dawn had come, Captain Andrés López Patiño and Captain
Martín Ochoa had already gone to discover the fort. When they
planned to attack, most of the people were incapacitated by the
water from the sky and from the land, and they had no light to see
what they were doing.*

*Thursday in the morning our good General was to attack with
his son-in-law Pedro de Valdes and Captain Patiño at his side. They
struck for the enemy fort with such a strong will that it did not
seem to meet any opposition at all. When the others saw this they
took spirit, and all did the same thing. It is to be noted that the
enemy did not come out at all until the attack began. As it was
morning and raining heavily in a great storm, most of them had
not yet arisen from their beds. Some came out naked and others
in shirts saying "I surrender, gentlemen." Notwithstanding this,
there was a slaughter of 142. Of the remainder of the settlement,
300 went fleeing by the walls and some went to the woods and
others precariously fled together to the vessels they had in the river.
In this way within an hour the fort was ours, without our side losing a man. There was not even one wounded.*

*There were six vessels in the river. They took for themselves a
brigantine and a galliot, although it was not finished. We took another vessel that was beached and discharged plenty of merchandise
from it. Of the other three, two were at the mouth of the bar to de-*

*fend the entrance, they believing we had to come by the sea. The
other was close to the port, loaded with wines and other things.
They did not wish to surrender if not given their ship. They shot
her from the fort to put her on the bottom.*

*Many good things were found in the spoils of war, 120 very
good corselets, 300 pikes, many arquebuses, many helmets, many
splendid cloth garments, much linen, many pants and shirts, many
fine light woolen stuffs, 200 pipes of flour, much sea biscuit, butter,
sheep and swine, although not too many, three horses, four asses
(2 females), 200 fanegas of wheat, oven and crushing mill, and
many other things which I leave for this time, God being pleased,
in order not to be prolix. The greatest victory which I feel for this
event is the victory which Our Lord has given us so that His Holy
Gospel may be planted and preached in these parts, where there is
so much need for it, for the liberation of souls that here were lost.*

*They found a great quantity of Lutheran books. They found
many packs of playing cards with the figure of the Host and Chalice
on the backs, and many saints with crosses on their shoulders and
other playing cards burlesquing things of the church. There died
among them a Lutheran who was a great mapmaker and necro-
mancer who had a thousand other bad things, and had been a Friar.*

*So today, Monday the 24th, at the hour of vespers, our good
General entered, accompanied by 50 foot soldiers, and they stum-
bled and were very tired, he and all those who came with him. The
news made known, I quickly went to my house and took out a new
cassock, the best I had, and a surplice and I took a crucifix in my
hands and went out to receive him at a distance before he arrived
at this port. He, like a good Christian gentlemen, before I reached
him, threw himself on his knees with all the rest that came with him,
giving many thanks to Our Lord for the great mercies received. In
this manner he was received with great rejoicing by us and we by
him. So great is his zeal and Christianity that all these works are
rest for his spirit. Certainly it appears to me that there could not be
human strength to endure so much, considering what he did. The
fire and desire he has to serve Our Lord in throwing down and
destroying this Lutheran sect, enemy of our Holy Catholic Faith,
does not allow him to feel weary in the work.*

*If we also wished to speak of his brother brought with him,
Captain Bartholomé Menéndez, I would never finish. He is no less
zealous in exalting our Holy Catholic Faith and obeying the com-*

*mands of his good brother, our General. When the General went out of this fort to attack the enemy, he left him in charge here, representing his own person. So great was the diligence that he showed all the time while his brother was away fighting that I never saw him undressed or lying in bed. He put sentinels on the land and sea at night and by day he occupied himself and all his soldiers in defenses and at other things at the fort. In the nights when we had alarms, plenty of them, the first man that came out completely armed with zeal to serve God and King, was him. The words that he said in the absence of his brother were sufficient to animate and console all his army so that even though they might have lacked provisions they would have fought like Romans.*

*Then if we should speak of the storms at sea, so valorous was the will of this good Captain that he greatly animated and inspired the pilots and sailors that they should do their duties in the times of peril we were in. Even when it was necessary to go aloft to the maintop for the assistance of those under his charge, he was the first to go. To avoid wordiness I will not go on with the things I have seen this man do, which certainly are all worthy of memory.*

*Then if you wish to question me about the Camp Master, he is a leading gentleman, son-in-law of the General and a very close relative of the Archbishop of Seville, a handsome young man of about twenty-five years of age, of very genteel presence, personable, strong-willed, diligent, educated in all things, especially in the things of war. For this reason the General always takes him at his side, and in capturing the fort and taking the enemy this good gentleman was the first that attacked them at the side of his father-in-law. In the slaughter that took place he was among those who most distinguished themselves. As the General observed how courageously he acted, he decided when he returned to the fort to leave him as Governor in the fort captured from the enemy. This he handled with much ability, working with his men to strengthen the fort, working a ditch around it and bastion toward the sea so that if half of France came it would not be enough to bother him.*

*On last Friday, September 28, some Indians came to this camp while the General was resting from the great work he had done. By signs they told us that toward the South there was a shipwrecked French vessel. At once our good General ordered the Admiral to fit a ship and take 50 soldiers and go up the river and out to sea to discover what there was. This done, two hours later the*

*General ordered me to be called to him and, as he has such great determination for this enterprise, he said to me, "Mendoza, it appears to me that I have not thought right in not having gone with those men." And I replied, "Your Lordship thought rightly and if your Lordship had tried to do anything else I and the rest of your servants would have prevented it to avoid the danger you might receive." While I was praising him more with words, his will would not allow it and presently he said he wished to go and he ordered me and certain Captains that were there to go with him. In all, we were up to a dozen men. We went in a boat after the company, with two Indians who guided us.*

*From here we went out of the river to go by the route of the sea in search of our enemies. We traveled more than two leagues by some level broken grounds; and ordinarily the water was about knee deep. The General was in front. After we came out of the water to the land we went about another three leagues along the shore, looking for our company. About ten o'clock at night we found them and we were all glad to be together. From there we could see the fires that the enemies made.*

*Our good General ordered two soldiers to go in the broken ground to reconnoiter the enemy and in view of their location to see what must be done against them. The soldiers went and in about two hours they returned and said that the enemy were on the other side of the river and that we could not get across to them. Then the General ordered two soldiers and four sailors to go back to where we left the boats to fetch them to where the enemy were. Later he commanded a march to the river and, before dawn, we arrived and in a broken ground hid ourselves together with the Indians we brought. When the day broke, we saw many of the enemy walking by the side of the river, fishing for shellfish to eat. After a little we saw them take out a banner and put in on a standard in the manner of war. Our good General who saw all this, enlightened by the Holy Spirit, said, "Gentlemen, I have decided to take off these garments and put on the habit of a sailor and take this Frenchman (who was one of those we brought from Spain) and go out and talk with these Frenchmen. Perhaps they are so broken that they may wish to surrender without fighting." As he spoke he acted. He began to shout and one of the enemy plunged in to swim and came over to talk with the General. He told the General of the wreck they had and how they were lost and that it* had been ten or twelve days since they had eaten a mouthful of bread. He also confessed that all or a greater part were Lutherans.

The General sent this one to return to his companions so that he might tell them on his part that they should surrender and bring their arms; and if not he would put them to the knife. In reply to this there came a French gentleman, Sergeant, and brought a message from the camp of the enemy in which they petitioned that the General would grant them their lives and that they would surrender their arms and give up their persons. After much parley between him and our General, the General replied and said that he did not wish to give such word but that they should bring their arms and their persons so that he should do with them as he wished, for if he gave them their lives he wished them to be grateful and if death they should not complain of his having broken his word. Seeing that they could not do anything else, the Frenchman returned to his camp. After a little time they all came with their arms and banners, and they entrusted them to his Lordship and put their persons in his power that he should do his will. Since they all were Lutherans, his Lordship decided to condemn them all to death. I, being a sacerdote and with the bowels of a man, petitioned him to grant me a favor, and it was that those whom he found to be Christians should not die. He granted me this, and proceedings were carried out by which we found ten or twelve. These we brought with us. All the rest died for being Lutherans and against our Holy Catholic Faith.

All of this transpired on Saturday, September 29, 1565, day of the Lord San Miguel. The number of Lutherans who died were a hundred and eleven men, except fourteen or fifteen we took as prisoners.

I, Francisco López de Mendoza Grajales, Chaplain of His Lordship, give faith that all of the above passed in reality and truth.

FRANCISCO LOPEZ DE MENDOZA GRAJALES.

# XII

# *Poems of Le Challeux*

ONE of the most interesting of the French colonists at Fort Caroline was the carpenter, Nicolas Le Challeux. In addition to writing a history of the colony after his return to France, he produced two poems. Challeux's history is well known, but his poems have never before been translated into English. In N. Le Challeux, *Deuxiem Voyage du Dieppois Jean Ribaut à la Floride en 1565*, edited by Gabriel Gravier (Rouen, 1872), the Editor's Preface has an account of Le Challeux—the writer-carpenter who left his shop, his wife, and two children when he sailed to the New World. The editor stated that the poems were not included in all editions of Le Challeux's work, but they were undoubtedly written by the carpenter.

### OCTET
(By the author when he arrived famished in his home in the town of Dieppe)

*Who wants to go to Florida?*
*Let him go where I have been,*
*Returning gaunt and empty,*
*Collapsing from weakness,*
*The only benefit I have brought back,*
*Is one good white stick in my hand,*
*But I am safe and sound, not disheartened,*
*Let's eat: I'm starving.*

### LITTLE LETTER
(Written by the author about the joy he felt when he saw Dieppe, his home town)

*Ha, I see you there, Dieppe, my beloved*
*Town which I have so longed for these days*
*But now you are in evidence*
*Before my eyes; therefore I hope*
*To go to see you more closely before the day is out.*
*Come on, my legs and feet, be ready*
*To carry me swiftly.*

164

*Hurry up, do your duty,*
*So that I may soon be at the place*
*Of Charity, to glorify God,*
*Listening to the preaching of His Word,*
*Sincerely, without frivolity,*
*By His Ministers, His faithful servants,*
*Who are for this His able scholars.*
*Not beguilers, but without taking away*
*Or adding thereto, they preach the Gospel*
*Openly, which is a noble thing to do.*
*Thanks to the Lord and to the Good King of France*
*Whom it pleased to give permission thereto;*
*And furthermore, as a Royal Prince*
*He showed his liberality to us*
*By giving us a good place for the adventure*
*With liberty to speak to the contrary.*

# XIII

# The Petition of the Widows and Orphans of Fort Caroline

WHEN he hanged the survivors of his attack on Fort Caroline, Menéndez spared the lives of women and children. Some eventually returned to France where they supposedly petitioned Charles IX for vengeance on the Spaniards. The petition was a Protestant remonstrance in the form of an open letter to the king and probably was prepared to benefit the religious and political aspirations of the Huguenots. The petition was translated by A. E. Hammond of the University of Florida and printed in the *Florida Historical Quarterly* (July, 1960), XXXIX, 55-61. Dr. Hammond's translation is reprinted by permission of the Florida Historical Society.

*Request[1] to the King, made in the form of a complaint,*
*by the widows, little orphans, friends and blood and marriage*
*relations of those that have been cruelly invaded by the*
*Spaniards, in Antartic France,[2] which goes by the name of*
*Florida.*

### To the King

*Sire, there is an endless number of poor and miserable people,*
*widows and orphans, all your subjects and vassals, who tearfully*

---

1. *The anonymous author of this letter appears to have produced numerous copies of it and to have distributed it for whatever propaganda effect it might have. It is preserved in the Bibliothèque Nationale in Paris. In the meantime, several editions have appeared in print, one of the earliest being that of Theodor de Bry, who produced it simultaneously in German and Latin in 1591 appended to the minor works of J. Lemoyne (Theodor de Bry, America [Part II, Frankfurt-am-Main, 1591]). It is also included in L. Cimber et F. Danjou, Archives Curieuses de l'Histoire de France (Paris, 1834-40, 27 vols.), VI, 232-37. In preparing this translation I have relied on the editions of Paul Gaffarel, Histoire de la Floride Française (Paris, 1875), pp. 477-81, and Suzanne Lussagnet (ed.), Les Français en Amérique Pendant la Deuxième Moitié du XVIᵉ Siècle (Paris, 1958), pp. 234-39.*
2. *This term has been erroneously employed. It was earlier used by André Thevet, Les Singularitez de la France Antartique autre nommée Amérique (Paris, 1558), to designate the parts of Brazil under French control. See Lussagnet, op. cit., p. 201, n. 2.*

*throw themselves at your majesty's feet, with the entire obedience
and natural submission which they owe you and bring to your excellency and highness a pitiful tale of their most just complaints
and grievances: or rather the sad spectacle and visible image of
their fathers, husbands, children, brothers, nephews, cousins and
relations by marriage, up to some eight or nine hundred men,
women and children alike, slaughtered and cut to pieces practically
to the last in this land of Florida, by Captain Petremelande[3] and
his Spanish soldiers. The more as this outrage is already odious
enough and all too villainous by itself, and as the blood of your
poor subjects, thus treacherously shed, cries to God for vengeance.
It behooves your majesty, Sire, to consider, if you please, that he
has made you sovereign King and granted you the obedience of so
many people to govern them with good laws and to uphold and defend them. Therefore the poor supplicants have no other recourse,
after God, but to implore your aid and protection and most humbly
entreat your majesty to succour, raise and sustain them: at the very
time when the wound of their anguish is still bleeding. In short, to
assist them with the same gentleness and consolation, as the em-
brace of a father to his own children, or the master's good face to
his loving and faithful servants: and, in fact, their complaints are
not less worthy of compassion and pity than the cruelty of the
Spaniard Petremelande is contrary to all war practices, and to all
laws and decrees that have been received either from God or from
men. And to explain it to you in full, your majesty, Sire, knows
well that your aforesaid subjects were sent by you in this land of
Florida, under your authority and by your express command, and
by virtue of your letters patent, in the form of commission and
leave, carried by Jean Ribaud:[4] the aforesaid vessels have arrived
in the aforesaid place in the land of Florida, were furiously invaded by five Spanish boats, the largest of which was eight hundred tons, the second two hundred tons and the others average ton-
nage. The people on board these vessels took first of all the fort
which had been built in your name by the French: and the men,
women and children found inside the aforesaid fort were murdered
and maimed by the aforesaid Spaniards without mercy. On the contrary, they displayed the pierced bodies of the little children held*

3. Pedro Menéndez.
4. *A more common spelling, in French documents, is Ribault.*

*on the point of their pikes[5] and secondly, they killed the aforesaid
Captain Jean Ribaud, and all his company of seven to eight hundred
men, in spite of the assurance and pledge they had given to spare
their lives, having bound their hands and arms behind their backs,
calling your subjects wicked, scoundrels, knaves, and French thieves,
and all this in the presence, and under the eyes, of the aforesaid Ribaud who, through horror of the aforesaid massacre, wanted
to come near the aforesaid Petremelande to place himself under his
protection, and nevertheless, the said Petremelande repelled him
and had him killed instantly by one of his soldiers, who struck him
a blow through the body with his dagger from behind, from which
blow the aforesaid Ribaud fell to the ground, and, once fallen, the
aforesaid soldier struck him another blow through the body from in
front, so that the aforesaid Ribaud remained dead on the spot, and,
which done, the aforesaid soldier cut off his head, shaved his beard
and split the head of the aforesaid Ribaud in four quarters, which
were stuck on top of four pikes in the centre of the place where the
other French people had died. Finally, the aforesaid Spanish captain sent a letter to the King of Spain, and enclosed in it the hairs
of the beard of the aforesaid Captain Jean Ribaud, in such a way
that the aforesaid Spanish Captain Petremelande and his men, in-
sulting with such brazen acts the servants of so powerful and renowned a King, want to make it plain that they set very little store
by honour, and fear even less the meeting of a mighty master. Your
majesty, besides, knows that, to complete the triumph of wickedness and increase the outrage of such an execrable crime: even
after death fun was made of, and mockery bandied at, the head and
beard of him who was no less a person than your lieutenant-gener-
al, and the paper of a letter was used as a dish to make a gift of the
hair of his beard. It is, however, incredible that there should be a
Christian, or even pagan, King or prince ready to own the aforesaid Petremelande after such a cruel and barbarous deed, surpass-
ing the rage and fury of Lions and Tigers, and the more execrable
as it was performed in a period of complete peace, truces and a*

5. *An obvious exaggeration. There exists no reliable eye-witness account of
this event by any Frenchman, Le Challeux, Laudonnière and Le Moyne having fled
Fort Caroline before the massacre. Spanish accounts specifically point out that
Menéndez had ordered all children under the age of fifteen and all women, re-
gardless of religious declaration, to be spared. See the account by Gonzalo Solís
de Merás in* Eugenio Ruidíaz y Caravia, La Florida, su Conquista y Coloniza-
ción por Pedro Menéndez de Avilés *(Madrid, 1893-4, 2 vols.), I, 87, 97, et passim.*

*friendly meeting arranged, while there was no war declared by you on any other nation or principality whatsoever, and nevertheless the Spaniards have set their hands upon places and people: which in no way belong to other than your Sceptre and crown: unless Petremelande chose to say that the strength of a foreigner can prevail against the King, to usurp what is yours, or to appropriate the power to command in your stead, or to give himself the authority of the letters and to take upon himself to punish and correct those that God has entrusted to you as subjects, with such a treasured wealth of submission, obedience and natural affection towards you, that they would rather die a thousand deaths, than deign to entertain the idea of changing masters, or voluntarily submitting to the yoke of another principality. If, therefore, Petremelande is disowned, his master has only to say that he is having, or will let you have, justice done, with such satisfaction and reparation as you are entitled to: in addition, forsaking and handing over to you the jurisdiction and possession of this land of Florida, which has long been acquired, occupied and held by your subjects in your name and under the title and authority of your Sceptre and crown, taking also into consideration that your aforesaid subjects have not been deported or relegated there as fugitives or deportees, but sent as ambassadors, officers and ministers of your majesty and as such recognized and owned by your letters patent commissioning the aforesaid Ribaud, held and acclaimed to act in these matters in the same capacity as you yourself, and no matter how atrocious such an indignity is by itself, yet it is made worse when left unpunished, and the dishonour is increased and the scandal carried further when the murders, violators of public faith, have their malice fed and sustained with impunity and can freely exercise it. Which your mansuetude, Sire, never allowing, will take up the quarrel of your poor subjects, thus unjustly outraged to the detriment of all laws, and with such great cruelty that it seems to be in order to dissolve the bonds of all human society, and break the divine order so thoroughly that the aforesaid Petremelande would, through his cunning, have all occasions for modesty lost, when patience is tried to the extreme.*

*The Carthaginians and African peoples have been strongly blamed for breaking their pledges in spite of all assurances given whenever this was advantageous to them. The Romans so faithfully observed theirs that they would keep them even to their enemies.*

*Would to God that the same tribute could be paid today to Petreme-lande and his fellow-countrymen, who have made so light of their promises and assurances and hypocritical solemn oaths impiously calling upon the name of God as though to make him a party to their treacherous disloyalty. If at times God uses the wicked ones, and allows them rope to give the full measure of their wickedness, as he did the Cananeans, he is not, however, subject to the strength of men, and, being stronger than them all, he fortifies the weaker and keeps us ceaselessly alive to our duty, that the thought of his gentleness and mercy does not make us forget the rigour of his justice and vengeance. So much so that, as in the same act, the crime of men is revealed, and the justice of God made manifest, so the warning befits them, that, it is said, God works in the hearts of the wicked as he pleases, yet pays each of them back according to their demerits.*

*To the King again.*

*Sire, you have heard what lamentations and regrets, what tears, or rather what dying sighs accompany the said memory of our misery and misfortune, the pitiful account of Petremelande's audacious and scandalous enterprise, the marks of his injustice and tyranny condemned by all laws; the tokens and memorials of his infidelity and treason, the intolerable contempt he showed for your authority and grandeur: in short, the murders and cruelties perpetrated against your servants and subjects, all or most of them virtuous and brave captains, men of honour and good repute, who would have acted as a living rampart around your majesty, and as frontiers to hold back all the enemies of your state. By which if there were ever humanity, compassion and mercy on record, the supplicants hope that our God in his goodness will so fill your heart with these, that your majesty will let himself be touched by our just grievances and pitiful complaints, will espouse our cause to see justice done, and, to that end, will extend to us his favour and pro-tection, which will be a pious work, worthy of your calling, and a manifestation of charity towards your poor subjects and faithful servants, with a view to assuaging the bitterness of their afflictions and bearing witness to their innocence to the whole of Christendom, which will make you beloved and hailed by all nations, not only as a King, but also as a father to your people.*

# XIV

## *Chief Saturiba, Ally*

ONE ADVANTAGE enjoyed by the colonists at Fort Caroline was the friendship of the Indians. Despite later difficulties with some native tribes, Laudonnière retained the good will of Chief Saturiba. A picture of the chief and a brief sketch of him are in André Thevet, *Les vrais pourtraits et vies des hommes* (Paris, 1584), Chapter 150, pp. 663 ff. This sixteenth century counterpart of a modern "mug" book (one with pictures and short biographies of outstanding contemporary persons) contains 150 biographies and pictures, and Saturiba's are the last ones in the book. Saturiba was an ally of Laudonnière, but Thevet's account relates to Saturiba, or Satouriona, and Dominique de Gourgues in 1568.

There is one notable historical inaccuracy in the writing; that is, stating that the Florida discovery was in 1512. In 1512 Juan Ponce de León secured a royal grant, with the title of adelantado, to conquer the island of Bimini to the north of Cuba, on the assumption that thereon lay the Fountain of Youth; but he did not set sail from Puerto Rico until March 3, 1513, and did not land on the Florida mainland until April 2, 1513, although his charter or legal right to make the discovery was in 1512.

In the museum at Fort Caroline National Memorial is an original sketch of Saturiba, which has been attributed by some authorities to the artist Jacques Le Moyne, a colonist in the Fort Caroline settlement. Also in the museum is a sixteenth century map reproduced from Le Moyne's original draft; this map shows the location of Saturiba's forces and other sites mentioned in the French text. Some of the most interesting Indian artifacts in the museum, including a Timuquan man effigy, were found on an island in Lake Kerr, clearly shown in the Le Moyne map as the location of Utina, another Indian chief mentioned in this article about Saturiba. These artifacts at the museum may well be objects used in the burial of Chief Outina.

171

André Thevet, *Les vrais pourtraits et vies des hommes* (Paris, 1584)

Saturiba, Laudonnière's ally

*CHIEF SATOURIONA, KING OF FLORIDA*

## Name and Discovery of Florida,
## and Where It Is Situated

Florida is fully acclaimed by the historians who have described its unusual qualities, holding the view that the flowers which she wears in her brow, always fresh and blooming, acquired

*for this country the name of Florida. It was discovered in the year
1512 by a Spaniard named Ponce de León who, seeking a fountain
of youth, discovered the mainland of Florida, which is a point of
land, similar to Italy, projecting into the sea more than 100
leagues; and the tip of it is 25 degrees of latitude from the Arctic
pole.*

## The River May

*This land teems with islands and rivers, among which the
River May is the most renowned, not only because it was discovered
by Captain Jean Ribault on the first day of May, which was why it
kept the name of May, but also because of its unusual character-
istics of which it has many. The impious and cruel acts which the
Spaniards visited upon this Norman captain were so numerous that
an account thereof could neither lessen nor remedy that bloody
score; although Captain Gourgues afterwards well revenged this
massacre, retaking from the Spanish Fort Caroline, which had been
built and named by him [Ribault] for his King Charles IX.*

## Satouriona Welcomes the French

*Rather than dwell further on this River May, I should intro-
duce here Chief Satouriona who is called by others Satiroa, a man
of great courage who had to cope with many and powerful adversaries and who was highly commended because of his open hospi-
tality extended to Captain Gourgues and his company.*

*He felt such affection for anything French that, having dis-
covered the fleet of Gourgues suddenly among them, he called out
from a distance "Antipola, Antipola." With all the kindness he
could show he made them the best welcome possible together with
two of his children, as handsome and strong individuals as one
could find anywhere. The older child was named Atore, a perfect
man in handsomeness, prudence, and honest countenance, one of
the most gentle, humane, and affable Princes who were in all this
country.*

## Some Kings of Florida

*After they had gone away together to exchange gifts and
friendly pleasantries, this King disclosed to the French captain what
enemies he had, namely Thimagoa and Olata Ouae Outina, two
very powerful Kings, to whom several others were pledged for assistance: Even Olata had vassals under him called Cadecha, Chilaly,
Esclauou, Eucappe, Calany, Onachaquara, Onittaqua, Moquoso,*

*and Aquera, besides Molona and more than forty others who were their allies and friends.*

*For his [Satouriona's] part it was not much trouble depending on this show of such a formidable force, not only for what he could do with them, but also for the help of thirty other chiefs which were under his command and of whom he was as sure as of his own people, due to the duty of alliance, confirming their loyalty, and also due to the hatred that the majority of them held against Olata Ouae Outina; and among others, Onatehaqua and Houstagna, powerful and wealthy lords, and principally Onatehaqua, who ruled over lands fertile and abounding in several crops. Above all others he made sure of de Potanou, a man cruel in war who had one thing particularly over the great Olata, namely the barrages of the hard stones with which he armed his arrows; and he [Satouriona] could not overcome his lands and dominions. As to his ten brothers, injury to Satouriona did not faze them, both because of this subjugation which bound them to stand behind any wrong done to their master and because of their family connection holding them together so closely that the plight of one became that of all the others. All his forces, as strong and as frightening as they were when unified, could not assure Satouriona of the victory that he wished to gain over his enemies, who were well united to put him down.*

### Lightning Strikes Out of the Blue
### Attributed to Burst of Naval Gunfire

*Nevertheless having observed this French fleet he considered opposing the power of Olata more for the natural prowess of a nation experienced in battle than because of the arquebuses they carried. These were so impressive for the poor barbarians that Chief Allycamany, having seen the marvelous havoc that lightning had made coming from the skies on August 29, sent to Captain Gourgues six Indians who, after they had presented some baskets of honey, pumpkins, and grapes, made known the desire which their Lord Allycamany [had] to establish friendship and alliance with him; though finding it strange in view of the obedience that bound him to the French, that they had set off against their abode the gunfire which had burned a great quantity of green prairies even up to the water line, approaching so close to his shelter that he thought he could see the fire in his own home. However this may be, the pagans were not more terrified of the lightning of Jupiter, than were these poor Floridians of the terrible explosion of the guns which belched forth fire; and I cannot but believe that Satouriona cherished and prized the assistance of the French on account of these pieces of ordnance in view of the hate that he later fancied against them, not only because of these thundering pieces but also for the refusal made by Captain Gourgues to escort them against Thimogoa, as he had promised him.*

### Captain Gourgues Refuses Aid to King Satouriona

*But he did not consider that Captain Vasseur, Lord d'Ottigny, and a few other Frenchmen were so greedy for the treasures which were in those parts, from which they had brought beautiful presents, and assurances of great wealth if they would be employed to aid a minor chief subject to the great Olata. This tied the hands of the French to such an extent that after holding out a long time their hand was forced in the end by Satouriona's discovery that they did not feel inclined to aid him. For this he was indignant. Finally he decided to go with the ten other chiefs against Thimogoa.*

### Ceremonies Held by Satouriona
### Before Going to War Against Thimogoa

*Before doing anything, he had water brought to him. This done, he set out to discuss many things and looked to the heavens, showing nothing in himself but a furious temper. Having done this for the space of half an hour, he poured with his hands on the heads of the ten chieftains some of the water which he was holding in a vessel, and threw the rest as in fury and spite on the fire, which had been quickly built there. After several other ceremonies he embarked and proceeded with such good speed with his fleet that the next day two hours before the sun set he arrived at the territory of Thimogoa, where he made a terrible massacre. His men carried away the heads of the enemies and cut off all the hair of their heads with a part of the scalp.*

### Satouriona Wins Victory Over Thimogoa

*They took twenty-four prisoners of which Satouriona took thirteen for his body guard. No sooner had Captain Gourgues heard of this than he sent a soldier requesting the sending of two of the prisoners to himself.*

## Captain Gourgues' Defiance of Satouriona

Satouriona refused this very arrogantly, which was the reason why he entered into the house of Satouriona with twenty soldiers without proper announcement, where he refused for half an hour to speak, then ordered the prisoners brought forward. After several delays Atore, son of Satouriona, went out to get them and brought them to Captain Gourgues who took them away in an off-handed way. Satouriona, very disturbed by this, sought means to avenge himself, concealing his ill feeling; but he sent messengers to the French with two full baskets of very large pumpkins. Among the Indians the French leader made it understood that he wished for means of accord between the people of Thimogoa and Chief Satouriona, which might turn out to be a great advantage to him [Satouriona], considering that by being allied with the kings of those areas it would make possible a passage to oppose Onathagua, his ancient enemy, whom he could not otherwise combat. In addition, the great Olata was so powerful that Satouriona could not break up his forces and undermine him, if he wished to be obstinate, but with the state of accord between the two they could easily ruin all of their enemies and push their boundaries to distant southern rivers. To carry out his promise he dispatched Captain Vasseur, Lord d'Arlac, and seven other soldiers to Olata Ouae Outina, to whom they returned their prisoners. This made him very happy, and also that they were to give a hand to Chief Ponano with a sailboat, which had loaded up at reveille in such quick fashion with two hundred of his men and our French riflemen in the lead that the victory was his.

# The Signature of Laudonnière

FOR YEARS after returning to France from Fort Caroline, Laudonnière followed the sea. Little is known of his activities after 1572, but a recently found manuscript shows that he was serving his king in 1573 as "Captain of the Western Fleet." This document has the only extant signature of Laudonnière, and is written in hand on vellum with an endorsement on its reverse side. The salary for the first quarter of 1573 was not paid until November of that year.

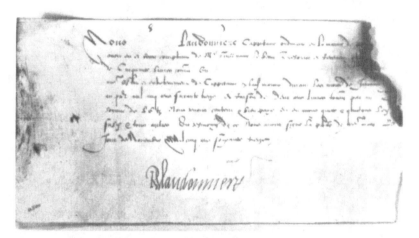

There is also acknowledged in this manuscript the prior payment of eight livres tournois on account. One livre tournois was one pound silver, minted at Tours, France. This document is now on display at the Fort Caroline National Memorial and reads as follows:

> 8. *Monsieur Laudonnière, regular Captain of the Western Fleet, declares to have received in cash from Monsieur Guillaume Le Beau, Treasurer of France, the sum of fifty livres tournois.*
>
> *Our Treasurer has advanced from the allowance of the Fleet Captain for the months January . . . in the present year one thousand five hundred and seventy-three, at the rate of two hundred livres tournois per year, the sum of 8 livres tournois which we have withheld and duly paid from the money due, quit and quittance,*

*signed, subscribed, etc. In witness whereof we have signed with our own hand . . . day of November one thousand five hundred and seventy-three.*

R. LAUDONNIERE

*[endorsement] By way of receipt for the sum of fifty livres tournois out of my budget, The Captain of the Western Fleet, for the quarter January, February, and March 1573.*

*to Capt. Laudonnière*
*city*
*January 1573*

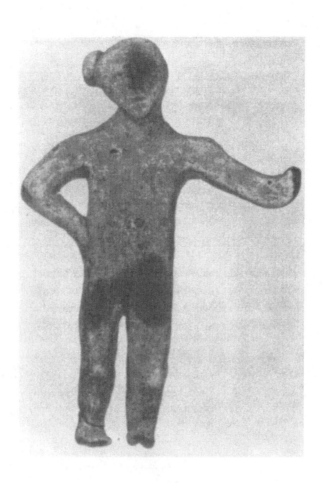

# APPENDIX A

# *The Heavens Direct*

HE bright, cool spray at the bow of a ship, nothing ahead but the sparkling sunny sea and adventure—thoughts like these have tugged at men and boys through history; and have at times made important history.

The reader today may wonder how Columbus and those who followed in the Age of Discovery found it possible to make such journeys at sea with very limited navigation instruments. What were the tools of the sea that Laudonnière used? The stars, the clouds, the sun, the moon, and the breezes—the heavens—were used for guidance.

Navigators of Laudonnière's time used a compass to tell direction and took readings on the sun, moon, and stars to determine latitude. In unknown and deep waters there was little else to rely upon except cloud formations to indicate land masses, and breezes to indicate speed.

Since the altitude of celestial bodies varies in different latitudes and the variations were then known, it was simple mathematics to find the latitude with the readings taken of the altitudes of celestial bodies.

The most sophisticated and important instrument for reading the altitudes was called the astrolabe. "Stripped of its astronomical complexities it was simply a flat ring of brass or other metal, graduated in degrees at whose centre was pivoted an arm, upon which were fixed two pinhole sights. It was provided with a swivelled ring through which the thumb was slipped when holding it to take an observation. The celestial body was observed through the sights, and its altitude read off the graduated ring. Two holes instead of one were often pierced in each of the sight brackets, the one small and the other somewhat larger. When the sun was bright, the astrolabe was held towards it and the arm was moved until the beam through the small hole in the foresight coincided with the small hole in the back sight. When the sun was dimmed by cloud or when an observation of a star was taken the sun or star was observed directly through the larger holes."[1]

1. J. B. Hewson, *A History of the Practice of Navigation* (Glasgow, Brown, Son & Ferguson, 1951), p. 71.

Photograph of a 16th century astrolabe recently acquired for the Fort Caroline National Memorial, Jacksonville, Florida. It is the only 16th century astrolabe in the Western Hemisphere of sufficient weight for navigational use.

Suspending the astrolabe by the thumb fixed its position with regard to the earth's surface and to take an observation on it was simple
enough. The astrolabe was invented by Hipparchus in 150 B. C. or
perhaps even earlier. However, it was originally used just on land. Martin Behaim is credited with adapting it as a navigation instrument in
1480. Columbus used it in 1492. It is still used for classroom instruction.
With a history of 2,000 years it can claim to be the oldest scientific instrument in the world.[2]

Another instrument introduced as a navigation instrument at about
the same time as the astrolabe was the cross-staff, also used to determine
latitude.

"It derived its name from its shape and consisted of a staff of wood
30 to 36 inches long and from $\frac{1}{2}$ to 1 inch in section. Upon this staff
cross pieces were fitted which could be moved along it at right angles.
Three cross pieces, or crosses as they were called, were usually supplied,
the shortest for use up to angles of 30°, the longer for angles between
30° and 60° and the longest for angles between 60° and 90°. Upon
the flat sides of the staff scales of altitude were cut with appropriate
crosses. To observe an altitude with it the 30°, 60° or 90° cross was slid
on the staff according to the angle to be measured, and the end of the
staff was held to the eye and rested on the eye bone. The cross was then
moved along the staff until its upper end coincided with the observed
body and the lower end with the horizon, and the altitude was read on
the appropriate scale where the cross intersected the staff."[3]

A mariner might well carry both the cross-staff and the astrolabe
on his ship. The cross-staff had no eye shield in those early days and
was not very useful in bright sunlight for this reason. Under certain circumstances it was adaptable to quick observations and in this respect
was probably preferable to the astrolabe in appropriate circumstances.
The astrolabe was much more usable in bright sunlight because of its
pinhole sights. These instruments may be dubbed the grandfathers of
the modern sextant.

Before discussing other navigation aids not quite so important in
uncharted seas, it might be well to mention something of the history of
the compass. The power of the magnet to attract iron was known in
Europe for several centuries before the Christian era. There are good
reasons to believe that the Chinese were the first to use magnetized iron
to indicate direction. It was used by them in navigation about A. D. 300
and by Europeans about A. D. 1000. The magnetic ore used was called

2. *Encyclopedia Brittanica* (Chicago, Benton, 1956), II, 575.          3. Hewson, p. 74.

the lodestone; and often mariners carried some with them to freshen the strength of their compasses.

"A certain amount of art was involved in sensitizing the needle. The pilot could either rub it on the lodestone before floating it, or, and this was more dramatic, he could float the needle in the bowl and then magnetize it by induction. To do this he held his lodestone close to the edge of the bowl: As the floating needle swung towards the stone he moved the stone round the bowl. Faster and faster he swung it until he was drawing the needle round too at a good pace. When he judged the right moment had come he snatched the stone away. Bereft of its attractive influence the needle stopped circling and settled in a north-pointing direction. Such actions smacked of wizardry to the uninitiated."[4]

Mathematics was not taught in many schools in those days because astrologers used mathematics and astrologers were supposed to be linked with the devil. Navigators had to know some math and know something of astronomy. Some, including Columbus, had an interest in astrology as well as astronomy despite the sinister reputation of the former.

For known waters the portolan charts were useful. They were first used to show the sailing directions, or portolani, and they looked at the world from the eyes of the navigator. Little attention was given to inland geography, but great detail was given on the chart relative to places on the coast, directions, distances, etc. No allowance was made on these charts for the converging of the meridians toward the poles; and each degree of longitude north and south of the equator was increased beyond its proper proportion. Courses run by ships were assumed in these charts to be on a flat surface. Some writers refer to these charts on the plane projection as plane, or plain, charts. During the Age of Discovery, navigators persisted in using this type of chart, although globes were available throughout the period and in 1569 Mercator published his famous projection map, which was not fully utilized until many years later. It was well into the eighteenth century before the plane charts became less popular. Refusal by pilots to use the better tool may have been calculated by them to retain an economic advantage of mystery in the profession.

An official in the Portuguese Embassy in Washington explained to the author that the navigation terms of "port" and "starboard" are derived from this period when the navigators often sailed from Portugal southward toward Africa and down the coast, relying on the portolani

---

4. D. W. Waters, *The Art of Navigation in England in Elizabethan and Early Stuart Times* (New Haven, Yale University Press, 1958), p. 22.

to show the course by known ports on the "port" side and the pilots having nothing to rely upon on the other side except the stars, hence the "starboard" of the ship.

Terrestrial globes and celestial globes were taken to sea on a few great expeditions, heavily financed ones of considerable significance, but they were not in common use at sea in the Age of Discovery. Neither was the armillary sphere, which gave land and celestial data on a series of circles and plates of metal.

A device which had use at sea but was probably not to be found on every voyage was the compendium or pocket dial. Sir Francis Drake's is on display at the National Maritime Museum, Greenwich, England. These compendiums contained such things as a sundial, compass, tide tables, tables of latitude, etc.

For the well-charted and known waters, the navigators helpfully used the oldest known navigation aid—the lead line. It is simply a weighted line to measure depth. The lead line was also helpful in protecting the ship in navigation in shallow depths, but it was never of much use to a navigator trying to find his way in unknown seas. It is mentioned in *Acts* 27:27-28 as follows:

"When the fourteenth night was come, as we were driven up and down in Adria, about midnight the shipmen deemed that they drew near to some country; and sounded, and found it twenty fathoms: and when they had gone a little further, they sounded again, and found it fifteen fathoms."

Finally, there was the log line to tell the speed of travel. The first certain evidence of a log line is in Magellan's voyage, January, 1521; but there is good reason to believe that use of this device was not characteristic of the Age of Discovery. Columbus and most of the others in the next 100 years, more or less, just sensed their speed from the breezes on their faces and did not measure speed with instruments. Despite its limited early use in the Age of Discovery, the log line was a product of the Age and so it is interesting for us to look at it and a few details concerning it. A log was thrown overboard at the time that a sand glass was tipped to record time. When 30 seconds had passed, the log was no longer allowed to distance itself from the boat and was pulled in. The length of the rope released during the 30-second interval gave the speed of the ship. The distance was measured in fathoms, that is, the length of the armspread of the man who brought in the rope. This was a physically convenient way to measure rope being brought aboard, but it obviously was not very accurate and was a varying measure depending upon the size of the man doing the job. The record of the speed was entered in a log book. The rope had knots tied in it at various spots for quick calculation and speed was thus measured in knots per hour. The modern term "knot" as a measure of speed measures nautical miles per hour and is a corruption of the word "nautical."

Some pilots of the Age of Discovery traveled by dead reckoning. This is the estimate of a ship's position solely from the distance run (calculated from the log) and the courses steered by compass, corrected for variations in current and leeway and without any astronomical observations. The term "dead reckoning" is probably a corruption of the phrase "deduced reckoning"—which later term was abbreviated in the columns of the early log books as "Ded. Reckoning."

J. Robertson in the *Elements of Navigation* (London, J. Nourse, 1754) listed the following allowances for leeway:

I. When a ship is close hauled, has all her sails set, the water smoother, and a moderate gale of wind, she is then supposed to make little or no leeway.

II. Allow one point, when it blows so fresh that the small sails are taken in.

III. Allow two points, when the top sails must be close reefed.

IV. Allow two and a half points, when one top sail must be handed.

V. Allow three and a half points, when both top sails are to be taken in.

VI. Allow four points, when the fore course is handed.

VII. Allow five points, when trying under the main sail only.

VIII. Allow six points, when both main and fore courses are taken in.

IX. Allow seven points, when the ship tries a hull, or all sails handed (bare poles).

Although from early times some navigators sailed without astronomical assistance, there were others from the very earliest records of navigation who used their knowledge of the stars to assist in navigation. Witness the Phoenicians, who in 600 B. C. used the Little Bear constellation and its relationship to the North Star as a constant guide in their journeys.

The Age of Discovery had no good way to ascertain longitude. One method used was to observe the difference in time of an eclipse of a star at a time when the time for that eclipse was known for another longitude. This would give the navigator the difference in longitude between the two spots. There were not enough known or observed eclipses to make this very useful as a procedure.

Philip III of Spain offered in 1598 a reward of 1,000 crowns for a satisfactory method of finding longitude at sea. Other countries followed suit. Finally in 1774 John Harrison collected the English award of 20,000 pounds for the development of a reliable watch which with one identifiable heavenly body and knowledge of latitude could bring an accurate finding of the longitude. The search for the method started in the Age of Discovery, but the method itself was 150 years in coming about as a practical procedure.

It would have been a great advantage to any country in the Age of Discovery to have an accurate method of finding longitude; because when the New World was being divided up among firstcomers, those who had accurate navigation instruments were at an advantage of great importance.

Great navigators of the time had a tendency to be somewhat international, as various countries vied for the knowledge they had or for their works. The famous John Cabot of England was a native of Italy, who served Italy, Spain, and England at various times. The same can be said for his son, Sebastian. And, of course, everyone knows that Columbus, an Italian by birth and residing in Portugal, found a sponsor for his talents in Spain at the important period of his career.

There is no evidence that René Laudonnière ever served any but the French; but there is a letter dated May 7, 1566, from the Spanish ambassador to the Spanish king indicating that Laudonnière sought employment by the latter in that year and that the ambassador had in mind a possible employment of him as an envoy; but all of this must be taken with some skepticism in view of the extreme anger that this same ambassador subsequently showed toward Laudonnière because of the Frenchman's loyalty to the reformed religion.

A navigator in the Age of Discovery looked to the Heavens for his chief guidance in more ways than one. His lot was not only to pilot ships but men and history, and, by God's will, the destiny of mankind for ages yet unborn.

# APPENDIX B

# Sixteenth Century Plant Life in Florida

RENCH and Spanish colonists in the sixteenth century were not generally good agriculturists. They sought valuable metals and other quick sources of wealth for their governments and often relied upon the governments back home or on the local Indian populations for food and supplies. The British were more inclined to agricultural pursuits in their colonies, perhaps learning this lesson from the failures of other nations.

The French at Fort Caroline did discover one plant that temporarily proved of value as an export. This was sassafras, valued as a drug. Dr. Nicholas Monardes, a doctor of Seville, Spain, in his book *Joyful Newes Out of the Newe-Founde Worlde* (London, E. Ailde, 1596, translated from a 1574 Spanish text by John Frampton) speaks of this as follows:

"It may be three yeeres past that I had knowledge of this tree and a Frenchman which had beene in those parts shewed me a peece of it and told me of the vertue thereof. He told me that the Frenchmen which had been in Florida at that time when they came into these parts had beene sicke the most of them, of grievous and variable diseases and that the Indians did shewe them this tree and the manner how they would use it and so they did and were healed of many evilles. . . . After the Frenchmen were destroyed, our Spaniards beganne to wax very sicke, as the Frenchmen had doone, and some which remained of them, did shewe it to our Spaniardes, and how they had cured themselves with the water of this marvellous tree. . . . The Frenchmen call it Sassafras. Our Spaniards call it after the same manner being taught by the Frenchmen."

Dr. Monardes gives case histories of people helped by this drug and mentions that Pedro Menéndez took samples back to Spain. Case histories of cures cited by Monardes include a variety of complaints, including headaches and infertility. The doctor says on the latter:

"Some women doo use of this water for to make them with child and in some it hath wrought the effect as it is well known. That which I can say is that gentlewoman being many yeeres married, without having children tooke this water, for that her husbande used it for certyne evils of depilations and of an ageive that held him with certaine fittes of a double certaine which he had and continued with the taking of it in the morning . . . keeping a good government whereby it came to pass that she was with child and brought foorth a sonne."

Another American plant used by the French at Fort Caroline as a drug, and found to be of commercial value, was tobacco. In addition to using it for lessening pain and reducing the pangs of hunger, the six-teenth century French used the plant in the curing of wounds and for colds in the head and for skin ulcers. Incidentally, the author has met people in rural Florida who have asserted that tobacco juice was effec-tive in lessening skin difficulties they had experienced.

Dr. Monardes' sixteenth century recitations on tobacco included the following: "Wormes, of all kinds of them is killeth, and expelleth them marvellously." He prescribed for this purpose tobacco "being taken in very little quantitie and the juyce thereof put on the navel."

Dr. Monardes reports that the word nicotine, for tobacco, came from the introduction of tobacco to the French court by Jean Nicot, the Queen's representative to the Portuguese court in the early 1560's. In France, Monardes reports, it was also called the "Queen Mother's herb," in honor of Catherine. (*See front and rear endleaves.*)

The drawings of Jacques Le Moyne as found in *Brevis Narratio* are primarily action pictures of events; but in the unobtrusive details of his drawings are observable many identifiable flowers, trees, vines, and shrubs. For the most part they are accurately and excellently drawn. In the edition of the *Illustrated London News* for February 10, 1962, there are shown some reproductions of Le Moyne paintings of European fruit, made after the artist had returned to Europe from Florida. The following comment accompanies the pictures:

"On December 11 last year an album containing fifty pages of water-colour drawings of flowers, fruit and vegetables, was sold at Sotheby's. . . . The Artist was a French Huguenot, Jacques Le Moyne de Morgues, who made a considerable name for himself in France, but fled to England in 1572 to escape the Massacre of St. Bartholomew. He was welcomed in this country and stayed here the remaining sixteen years of his life. Several noblemen gave him their patronage: among them no less a person than Sir Walter Raleigh, who offered him lodg-ings in Blackfriars and also took him into his service. The Sidney family also helped him and to the Lady Mary Sidney, mother of Sir Philip, he dedicated his *La Clef des Champs*, illustrated with woodcuts. . . . There is only one other known collection of drawings by Le Moyne de Morgues in existence. This album is also of flowers and fruit and was made by the artist before his flight to England. . . . A number of the woodcuts in Le Moyne's book *La Clef des Champs*, crude though they are in comparison with the artist's original water-coloring, were based on the earlier collection. . . . Le Moyne de Morgues was an artist of exceptionally high accomplishments and sensitivity."

The book *La Clef des Champs* was printed at Blackfriars in London in 1586 and the only known copies of it are in the British Museum.

# INDEX

Africans: on 1564 expedition, 17, 72, 89; difficulties with some of them, 26, 72; Menéndez feared uprisings of, 43

Alexander VI, Pope, divided the "unknown world," vii, 80

Alligators, flying, 74

Amboise, Treaty of, ended the first French religious civil war, 16

Bison, at Fort Caroline, 21, 59 n14

Calvin, John, 5

Cartier, Jacques, financed by France in early American explorations, 4

Charles IX: Catherine de Medici ruled in name of, during his youth, 5; Charlesfort named for him, 15; Fort Caroline named for him, 19; met Spanish ambassador after fall of Fort Caroline, 46; friend of Coligny, 51; allowed Coligny to be murdered, 51

Charlesfort, South Carolina: established, 15, 81; abandoned, 16, 81, 120; Rouffi left at, 107

Coligny, Gaspard de: leader of Huguenots, 6; reaffirmed in power with Catherine, 16; chose Laudonnière as leader of 1564 expedition, 17; retained in power, 49, 51; murdered, 51

Criminals, at Fort Caroline, 72

Cross-Florida channel, believed by some Frenchmen to exist, 92

Elizabeth I, Queen of England: negotiated with Ribault, 15; imprisoned him, 15

Fort Caroline: purposes of the colony, 13, 14, 17, 22; composition of colony, 17, 19, 20-21; beginning of construction, 19; named for Charles IX, 19; nature of construction, 19-20; religious services at, 21, 27-28; wine made at, 21; amusements at, 21; children born at, 21, 132; food shortage, 21-22, 28; reinforcement by Bourdet, 22; romantic alliances with Indian maidens, 25, 26, 72; mutinies at 30, 91, 103; assisted by Hawkins, 31; reinforced by Jean Ribault, 33; captured, 38; significance of, 44; criminals at, 72; Africans at, 72, 89; women at, 89, 100; petition of widows of, 166

Gold: a purpose of Fort Caroline, 22; search for by Laudonnière, 22; gold trinkets bartered from Indians, 23; gold mines located in the "Apalatcy" mountains, 23, 60 n15; Laudonnière refused to reveal to Hawkins, 54; colonists had, with silver and pearls, 96

Gourgues, Dominique de, 48-49, 171

Grajales, Francisco López de Mendoza, 141

Guise, Francis, 2nd Duke of: took power from Francis II, 5; became a hero for slaughter of Protestants at Vassy, 6; held Dieppe in 1562, 16; assassinated, 16

Guise, Henry, 3rd Duke of, 51

Havre-de-Grâce: departure port for 1562 expedition, 14; departure port for 1564 expedition, 65

Hawkins, Sir John, 31

Huguenots: controlled a number of

French cities, 5; held first national synod in 1559, 5; furnished most of participants in 1562 voyage, 14; predominated in 1564 voyage, 17

Laudonnière, René de Goulaine de:
—*youth and ancestry*: origin of name, 7; family background and landholdings, 7; birth, 7; a Huguenot, 7; relative of and assistant to Coligny, 7
—*navigation prior to 1564*: voyage to Algeria, 9; captured by the Spanish, 9; seagoing wardrobe and possessions, 9-10; served various French monarchs, 10; Ribault's lieutenant in 1562, 13
—*founded and governed Fort Caroline*: began the permanent settlement of what is now the United States, viii; was first to lead a colony of men and women dedicated to religious freedom in our land, viii; chosen to lead the Fort Caroline expedition, 17; built Fort Caroline, 19; Vale of Laudonnière, 19; transactions with Indians, 21-22, 29; accused of improper alliance with his chambermaid, 26-27; ruled with iron hand, 28-29; protected the poultry flock for the colonists, 28; his life was plotted against, 29, 73; escaped Fort Caroline at its fall, 38
—*later years*: returned to France 41, 45; wrote book, 46; reported to Charles IX, 47; at center of revenge plots, 48; trip to West Indies, 49; contract on later trip to America, 50; "The Captain of the Western Fleet," 52, 177; evaluation of, 53-59; law suit and last residence, 60 n31
Le Challeux, Nicolas, 39, 87, 164
Le Moyne de Morgues, Jacques: characterized Laudonnière, 28; an outstanding artist, produced books, 187-88

Manrique de Rojas, Captain Hernando de, 34, 107
May, River of, discovered, later named St. Johns, 14
Medici, Catherine de: originally persecuted heretics, 5; gave Huguenots limited freedom, 5-6; met Spanish Ambassador after fall of Fort Caroline, 46-47; planned new Protestant persecutions and Coligny's murder, 51
Meleneche, Robert, deposition of, influenced decision of Menéndez to attack by land, 36
Memyn, Jehan, 99
Mendoza Grajales, Francisco López de, 141
Menéndez de Avilés, Pedro: sent by Philip II to conquer Fort Caroline, 35; founded St. Augustine, 35; captured Fort Caroline, 37-38; letters of, 127, 130; his priest's diary on the conquest of Fort Caroline, 141-163
Monsters, 31, 71, 74-75
Moors. *See* Africans
Morgues, Jacques Le Moyne de. *See* Le Moyne de Morgues, Jacques

Negroes. *See* Africans

Outina, 29, 171, 173, 176

Pensacola, settled in 1559 and abandoned two years later, 12
Philip II: issued decree in 1561 against further Spanish settlement north of Mexico, 12; sent Menéndez to capture Fort Caroline, 35, 125; laughed at St. Bartholomew's Day massacre, 51; order of, 125; letter of, 126
Ponce de León, discovered Florida, 12, 171

Reformation, the: effect upon European outlook, 4; followed by Counter Reformation, 4
Religion: freedom of, a motive for colonization, 13; services at Fort Caroline, 21, 27-28
Ribault, Jean: led 1562 expedition to America, 14; negotiated with Queen Elizabeth and imprisoned, 15; wrote book, 15, 64; reinforced Fort Caroline, 33; death of, 42
Ribault, Jacques, 33, 41, 47, 48
Rojomonte, Stefano de, 94
Rouffi, Guillaume, 107

Saint Bartholomew's Day massacre, 51

Sassafras, considered as a medicine and as a product for commerce, 25, 186

Saturiba: helped Fort Caroline colonists, 23, 29; Thevet's biographical account of, 171

Serpents, flying, at Fort Caroline, 71

Sex, a problem at Fort Caroline, 26

Tobacco: used at Fort Caroline, 21, 31; considered as a medicine and as a product for commerce, 25, 187

Unicorns at Fort Caroline, 31

Vassy, 6

Verrazano, Giovanni da: financed by France in early American explorations, 4; founded France's claims to Florida, 13

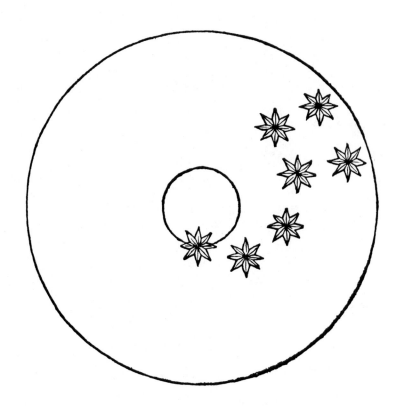